In pr

"Ironman brought bac}   'g
the game from my Dad ana big brother, that sound of wood smacking
the rawhide, that glorious but sad '69 year with its ups and downs. As
a young pitcher, what a thrill it was for me to be pitching to one of the
premier catchers in the big leagues. His skill behind the plate, knowledge of the hitters, connection to his pitchers, and a great arm really
put me at ease on the mound. If you love the game of baseball, the way
it used to be played, for love not money, you'll love this book!"

Richard Nye MLB 1966–1970 (Cubs, Cardinals & Expos)

"I had the good fortune to play with Randy on the Minnesota Twins
back in 1974. We've enjoyed playing golf in celebrity tournaments
over the years, and I often tease him about his refusal to utter a cuss
word, while substituting the usual verbiage for things like "shucks"
"gosh dang" or "bloomin' fanny." It's quite the contrast to the hard-
nosed, fiery player he was back in his playing days, and the kind and
gentle man that everyone has come to love. Enjoy this book, and the
stories from his big years with the Cubs, and the great legacy he carved
out in baseball."

**Eric Soderholm MLB 1971–1980 (Twins, White Sox, Rangers
& Yankees)**

"Want to know a secret a father told his eight-year-old son and then
taught him how to use that secret? Want to know how that secret
took him all the way to the major leagues where he became one of the
premiere catchers in baseball? Want to know how that secret helped
him win a Gold Glove award? Want to know about a man who holds
the record of catching 160 games in a 162-game season? Want to read
about a good man who achieved greatness through hard work and
determination? His name is Randy Hundley and it's all in this must-
read book."

Tom Dreesen Comedian/Author/Actor

IRONMAN

IRONMAN

LEGENDARY CHICAGO CUBS CATCHER

RANDY HUNDLEY

WITH JOHN ST. AUGUSTINE

FOREWORD BY Ferguson Jenkins

AURORA PUBLISHING
2023

First Printing: August 2023

ISBN **978-1-312-42717-4**

Photo/image credits: Licensed Getty Images pgs. 76, 89, 90, 91, 93, 94 113. The Hundley family archives pgs. 8, 9, 13, 24, 27, 29, 31, 78, 84, 110, 129, 130. Randy Hundley Fantasy Camp pgs. 4, 150, 156, 160, 162, 172, 188. Chicago Cubs pgs. 37, 67, 87, 97, 101, 107, 115, 117, 127, 140, 177, 181, 182. Roanoke Times pgs. 15, 23. Bob Sirott pg. 167. Murray Olderman used by permission pg. 51. Topps pgs. 34, 40. John St. Augustine pg. 20.

Contents

OUR THANKS TO...

FERGUSON JENKINS

JODY DAVIS

RICH NYE

ERIC SODERHOLM

TOM DREESEN

JULIE HUNDLEY HERMANSON

RENEE HUNDLEY IGNOFFO

KENN HUNDLEY

THE HUNDLEY FAMILY

JENNIFER GEIST

LORI SOCKI

BETH CHAPLIN

JOHN WROBLEWSKI

GEORGE CASTLE

PATTY CULLITON

TERESA RODRIGUEZ

GARRY PRANGE

THE CHICAGO CUBS

FOR BETTY

FOREWORD

BY FERGUSON JENKINS

In all of sports, there isn't a more intimate relationship than the one between a pitcher and a catcher in baseball. These are the only two players in the game that are in on every single play. It becomes a dance of sorts, knowing what pitch to throw to a certain batter, based on his tendencies and game situations. Long before the season begins, pitchers and catchers spend hundreds of hours together, throwing the ball back and forth, perfecting their cadence and communication, much of it unspoken. Then during the season, in the heat of the game, those early innings in spring training become so very important.

In my 19 years on the mound, no one caught more of my games than Randy Hundley.

Out of 664 total games pitched, he caught 188 of them, including 17 of my 49 shut-outs. Over my career, I've had some formidable backstops, like Hall of Famer Carlton Fisk with the Red Sox and Cubs' catcher Jody Davis, as well as Jim Sundberg with the Rangers. But none of them had the same effect on my game that Randy did, perhaps because we went so far back when we both came to the Cubs in 1966. Randy from the SF Giants, and I was traded to Chicago from the Phillies.

Initially, I was in the bullpen with the Cubs, and I watched how Randy (young as we were) handled the pitching staff like a veteran player. When I would come in relief, I had every confidence that he and I would be able to work the game situation to our advantage.

But it didn't always go our way.

In 1966 we lost 103 games and finished 10th in the National League. Back then, the Cubs were on a serious learning curve under Leo Durocher, who eventually moved me into the starting rotation and that's when things really began to get interesting. In 1967 I had my first of six consecutive 20-game winning seasons and made the All-Star team. Much of my success was due to Randy being behind the plate. As I said back in 1970 … *"Having Hundley catch for you was like sitting down to a steak dinner with a steak knife. Without Randy, all you had was a fork."*

He was right there with me when I won the NL Cy Young Award in 1971.

This is a guy who revolutionized the game of baseball with his one-handed catching style and holds the record for most games caught in a single season, as well as racking up a serious fielding percentage over a 14-year career. He played through injuries that would have ended a lesser player's career and when Leo gave him full reign over the on-field game, Randy became the sparkplug that kept the Cubs moving forward. We had a four-man rotation back then, each of us pitching on three day's rest, but the one constant presence behind the plate was Hundley, and it made all the difference knowing he was back there.

Those Cubs teams were loaded with talent just waiting to come together, and to go from last place in '66 to being in first place for 155 games in '69 was a tribute to what happens when you put the right people in the right positions and keep giving it everything you got. While we came up short in 1969, that season forged a bond between those of us who played that year, and the fans in Chicago that have always showered us with love and respect, even though we didn't win it all.

Back in 1983, Randy asked me to participate in his first fantasy camp. I was still pitching after being traded back to the Cubs from the Rangers in 1981. To be in the locker room again with Ron Santo, Glenn Beckert, Ernie Banks, and Randy running it all, was a real gift. It didn't take long being on the field with the campers for me to see how important the camp concept was to legions of Cubs fans, who were having the experience of their lives.

The success of the fantasy camps comes as no surprise, as Randy approached it as he did his time in the big leagues, with great purpose and passion, wanting the rookies wearing pinstripes to understand from top to bottom what the game of baseball is all about. While he never made it to the majors as a manager, there is no doubt in my mind the fantasy camps became his team for 38 years, which is an incredible achievement.

This book chronicles the journey of a country boy to the big city, his incredible connection with the Chicago Cubs, and his singular place in the game. When you think of the thousands of players who have played in the major leagues, most of their names are forgotten, but there is one name—*Randy Hundley*—that will forever be remembered as the man who caught more games in a single season than any other catcher in the history of the game and played hardnosed baseball to the final pitch.

He's truly an "ironman" in every sense of the word.

Ferguson Jenkins
National Baseball Hall of Fame (1991)
MLB 1965–1983 (Philadelphia Phillies, Chicago Cubs, Texas Rangers, Boston Red Sox)

INTRODUCTION

This book is a long time coming, I'm here to tell you.

Over the years I've watched my former Chicago Cubs team-mates share their experiences between the covers of a book, (I wrote the foreword to Fergie's) and have read many sports books with memories and more about this storied franchise, especially the 1969 season. The stories have kept our team in the headlines for the past 54 years, ever since we came up short and lost out to the "Miracle Mets." We've been called "lovable losers" and "the greatest second-place team in the history of baseball" among other things, which I suppose is true on some level, but there is so much more to that time than our deep dive at the end of the year.

I've always wanted to share the memories from my years in the game, and I'd been waiting until the time felt right. When I turned 80 years old in 2022, I figured it was getting to the "*now or never point*" to tell my story. I reached out to my longtime friend and best-selling author John St. Augustine and asked him to help me put on paper what has long been on my mind and in my heart. Big John attended our Wrigley Field Fantasy Camp back in 1993 and hit a grand slam (which he's been living off ever since) and I knew I could trust him to help me share my experiences in the most authentic way possible. My journey has taken me, a skinny 17-year-old kid from little Bassett High School in Virginia, to the majors as a catcher with the San Francisco

Giants, Cubs, Twins, Padres, and back home to Chicago to finish my career. Along the way, I earned a coveted Gold Glove Award, became an All-Star, and spent time with some of the greatest players and characters the game has ever known. Also, because of my dad, I was the first one-handed catcher in the history of baseball, a move that totally changed the game from behind the plate.

As a catcher, I had a very different view of the game than any other position player, a perspective that was enhanced after being installed as the "field general" for the late, legendary Hall of Fame manager Leo Durocher, during the most crucial years of our team in the 1960s and early 1970s. In my opinion, playing catcher is the most challenging position in the game, as you are calling pitches, setting up the defense, keeping an eye on the batter as well as the base runners, sometimes in extreme heat, wearing all that gear, day after day, and trying to maintain a respectable batting average at the same time. Add to that, the nagging injuries that come with playing a few thousand innings of baseball in the squatting position, and the pressure of never knowing when an injury or the hands of time will end your career.

I loved every minute of it.

The game has changed in many ways since I played. The players today are bigger, faster, stronger, and wealthier than in my time. Back then, we'd all work the "chicken dinner circuit" which consisted of a speaking engagement, maybe $50 for our time, and an all-you-can-eat chicken dinner to top it off. Most, if not all, of the guys I played with in the 1960s and 1970s had offseason jobs to help make ends meet. Today, the salaries are in the millions and many players have lucrative endorsement deals. I think I was paid a few hundred dollars for doing some bank commercials, but that's about it. I'm pretty sure none of the guys I played with (or against) back in my day, had a private jet, trainer, or shoe deal. Back then no one lifted weights or did anything more than stretching. These days the players are built like football linebackers and are incredibly strong, and it seems a 100 mph fastball is the norm. They have wireless devices to call pitches, coaches can challenge calls, and someone in New York can overturn a play, effectively changing the trajectory of a team and perhaps a season. Launch angles, exit velocity, and sports analytics dominate the game. It seems like we need to be endlessly entertained, and the fan "experience" in some ways overshadows the game of baseball itself.

Much of my career was during the 1960s, which might just be the most volatile decade I can remember. Those years playing baseball through times of major unrest in our country, while the war in Vietnam raged, a president and leaders were assassinated, and riots in the streets were commonplace, was often a challenge. Additionally, civil rights didn't always extend to many of the players of the day, no matter how big of a star they were on the field. Off the field, they were treated like second-class citizens, even though they were first-rate ballplayers. Segregated road trips were the norm, and it was painful to watch my teammates of color treated in such a way.

However, through it all, I began to understand the importance of the game during turbulent times. Baseball was the perfect distraction from the bad news that loomed outside of the stadium, which in turn became a safe haven for fans, who just wanted a sense of normalcy, a chance to sit in the sunshine and cheer on their hometown heroes, and to forget the terrible headlines, if only for a few hours.

Ironman is a road map of my time in the game, starting with my childhood and teen years, then onto wearing #9 with the Chicago Cubs, which of course includes the 1969 season, and what it was like to see that great team broken apart. My own trade from the Cubs, overcoming injuries and then returning back to Wrigley one more time, which was the perfect capstone to my 14-year playing career. The long run of my baseball fantasy camps and the thrill of being inducted into the Chicago Cubs Hall of Fame, as well as being honored with a World Series ring.

The process of writing this book had me reliving so many great moments, and I am honored and excited to share them with Chicago Cubs fans, the greatest in all of baseball!

-1-
The Mitt

For as long as I can remember, I wanted to be a baseball player. It was a passion for the game I was born with; it took hold of me as a little boy and has never left me, all these decades later. The sights, sounds, and excitement of baseball have always been with me, it seems. But there was no way to know when I was just a kid how far it would actually take me.

When I was about six years old, we lived close to a baseball diamond, and I can clearly recall being in a pickup game with much older boys. For some reason they stuck me in left field, which is the last place you would put a kid who was a rookie. It didn't take long for a high fly ball to be hit in my direction, and, shading my eyes from the sun with my glove, I measured the tiny speck in the sky that got *bigger* and *bigger*, and with a loud *thump* caught the ball in my glove, cradling it against my chest.

I knew then and there that baseball would be my life.

The Hundley Family—1960

****

Growing up in Martinsville, Virginia, back in the 1950s was as down-home as it gets. I'm the oldest, then my sisters, Mary Lois and Pat, with my brother, Kenn, as the youngest. My dad, Cecil, was a hardworking man, whipcord strong, who would fight for his right to be heard, at the drop of a hat. To say he had a short fuse would be putting it mildly. Dad didn't weigh more than 155 pounds on a good day, and if he needed a sizeable stick to get his point across to bigger men, he wasn't opposed to using it. He was an aircraft fabricator during WWII and eventually owned the Cecil R. Hundley Construction Company Inc., which was a very demanding career, but he always found time to watch baseball on TV. My mom Lois was the counterbalance to his hard-edged personality and was very supportive of me in every way. As children, we learned the simple values of faith and family, which continue to be mainstays of my life. I also learned the value of hard work, as I watched my dad's construction company build the now-famous Martinsville Speedway, which was the first paved oval track and is also the shortest track on the NASCAR circuit. I recall the time when I was about eight years old, and, wanting to imitate my dad at work, I jumped into a road grader and somehow got the thing moving, ending up in a ditch. My dad was at first relieved I was okay, then mad that I did it, but underneath, I could tell that he was proud of my first outing as a heavy-equipment operator.

It was a post-war life for us, and the 1950s was a time of prosperity, the "boom" that included a robust economy, development of suburbs, and even rural America was on the rebound after WWII. My days were filled with school and friends, baseball whenever possible, and listening to ball games on the radio—I couldn't get enough of it.

Eventually, I attended John D. Bassett High School, and of course played baseball all four years, along with two years of basketball (as a guard on the state championship team as a junior) and football. Actually, I was the starting QB, until I decided to opt out of football my senior year, when I was also named "Most Athletic Boy."

While there was much going on in the world, my only focus was on baseball. There's no question that my love for the game comes directly from my dad, who was a semi-pro catcher for more than 20 years and wore the *"Tools of Ignorance."* It's a term coined by catcher Herold "Muddy" Ruel, who played on eight different teams from 1915 through 1934. Muddy was pointing out the irony that a player with the smarts needed to be an effective backstop, would be stupid enough to play a position that required so much safety equipment. My dad sorta proved that point. As a two-handed catcher, he constantly got nicked by foul tips and paid the price to the tune of 26 broken bones in his right hand. His catching skills were good enough that prior to working on aircraft, he was offered a contract to play pro ball by the Baltimore Orioles. He turned it down, knowing that being on the road and away from my mom and me would never work out. Outside of playing semi-pro, my dad continued his passion for baseball by coaching the Connie Mack Martinsville Pirates for many years, helping young players develop their skills. I've heard from many of his former players about the positive impact he had on their lives and how they learned to appreciate the lessons the game offers, all because of his influence.

Back in the day, my dad played against the great Stan Musial in semi-pro ball and that made him a serious St. Louis Cardinals fan (something that later in my career would always be an interesting conversation, seeing that the Cubs/Cards rivalry is one of the greatest in baseball.) By the time I was eight years old, I was playing shortstop in Little League, and because I had a pretty good curve ball I was also in the pitching rotation, which I really enjoyed. I had one of those big arc curves that starts out above your head and then drops across the plate like a shot. It used to scare the crap out of the opposing batters, but like many young players, being on the mound can ruin young arms, and after half a season, my dad intervened and made his thoughts known about the dangers of pitching those looping curves for too long.

I took his words to heart and got off the mound. What now? I moved back to shortstop for a bit because I knew I had a strong arm, but it just didn't feel like I fit in on the diamond. As I watched my friends find their positions on the field, I wanted so much to be part of the game, but not knowing my place in it was really difficult for me.

Not long after, on a Saturday afternoon, I walked into our family room, and my dad was lazing on the couch, watching a ball game. I summoned up my courage and said, "Dad, I'm not having any fun at shortstop, and you don't want me to pitch. Where else is there for me to play?"

My dad looked at me, turned off the ball game (which rarely happened), and without saying a word, pointed in my direction, and I followed him to the front door. Just as we get ready to go outside, he turned to me, put his big finger in the middle of my forehead, right between my eyes, and said, "Randy, I am going to teach you to be a catcher. But you are going to learn how to be a one-handed catcher, *and if I ever see you put that bare hand up to catch a ball, I'm coming to get you!"*

I knew that my dad meant every single word of it.

Back then being behind the plate was a two-handed posi-

Cecil Randolph Hundley Sr.

tion because the mitts were big and stiff, like an old leather seat cushion. He was determined that I would learn to catch one-handed to keep my fingers intact because a catcher with busted digits can't throw out base-stealers.

From the moment I squatted down in our front yard with my dad's big, heavy mitt on my left hand, with my right hand tucked safely out of the way, I knew deep down inside that this was my place in the game. With every smack of the ball in that big mitt, the feeling went deeper and deeper, as my dad pitched faster and faster. He bounced in a few, just so I could learn to block the ball. It took some getting used to because the natural thing was to put my right hand up to the mitt, but every time I made that move, my dad would stop and look at me until my hand was safely behind my leg and out of harm's way. My dad and I played catch until it got too dark to see the ball. I slept that night with a feeling of connection to both my dad and the game, as I never had before. In Little League, I began catching one-handed while wearing my dad's mitt.

It was in that front yard, with my dad, that would set the course for my life as a professional baseball *catcher*, who besides the pitcher is the only player involved in every play. He's the sparkplug of the team, the guy who directs not only the pitches thrown, but has to be the leader from behind the plate, and in many ways, the on-field manager. I couldn't wait to put the gear on for games and would practice catching "pop-ups" in the yard for hours, throwing the ball up as high as I could, and camping out underneath it, as if a batter had hit a high foul ball.

****

Not long after my first lessons from my dad, I was walking home from school and wandered into a nearby department store that had a small sporting goods section. There, among bats and balls, hats and spikes, was a hinged catcher's mitt! I couldn't believe it! I tried it on and it fit my hand like it had been sewn *just for me!* I must have stood there with that mitt on my hand for nearly half an hour, pounding my fist into the pocket, admiring the hand-stitched leather. Not having any money to purchase it, I buried it among the other mitts and gloves in the pile, hoping no one else would see it. Every single day after school, I'd stop by to see if someone had bought it, and I kept hiding it among the other sports gear, moving it in rotation around the store, in an attempt to keep it from being sold.

This routine went on for a couple of weeks, until one day, the department store manager (who had been watching me the whole time) called my dad and said, "Mr. Hundley, you have got to come down and buy this mitt. Randy has been by here every day after school and keeps rearranging the sporting goods section, to make sure no one finds it but him." It was an expensive mitt, a Wilson brand Frank House signature model A2402, with the "Grip Tight" pocket. (House was a catcher with the Tigers, KC Athletics, and Reds.) At that time, it cost well over $100, and my dad wasn't made of money. But somehow, he found the funds, and with a break on the price from the department store manager, I had my first catcher's mitt!

It was a beautiful mitt. I used it through a couple of seasons in Little League, then Pony League, and then in high school ball. It was my most prized possession and was a signal from my dad (who was a man of few words) that he loved me and was solidly behind my dreams of becoming a big-league catcher. I took care of that mitt, making sure to

Bassett High School — 1960

keep the laces tight and the pocket well-oiled. Back then, in the offseason, I would take a nice dollop of Vaseline, smear it in the pocket, put a ball in there, and wrap the whole thing tight with a belt. Then, I'd put the mitt under my bed for safekeeping, and once the season started up again the pocket of that mitt was good to go. If you have played baseball at any level, you know how important that first glove or mitt is. All these years later, my first catcher's mitt remains my favorite and is still in the Hundley family.

Baseball season was a busy time for my dad and me. He always found the time to be at every game I played in, and I would follow his semi-pro games on the weekends when he was behind the plate. You can imagine how I felt when my dad would be watching me catch a game during the week, and then I would be behind the fenced backstop on the weekend, watching him doing the very same thing.

Those were glorious days.

His presence was an example to me of what it meant to be an effective backstop, to take charge of the pitcher and the game, and to not take any crap from the umps. My dad hit left-handed, and while not a big man, used a bat the size of a fence post and could hit the ball a country mile. There is an article from the *Roanoke Times* dated July 4th, 1950, that reads: "*Cecil Hundley, of Martinsville, smacked a 470-foot home run in the 3rd inning against Rocky Mount.*" He played hurt most of his career, due to that two-handed style that was the norm back then, which made him adamant that I would catch one-handed.

His influence on me was so great that even when I had made it to the majors, I'd always hear his words in my head. *"If I ever see you put that bare hand up to catch a ball, I'm coming to get you!"*

When I broke into the big leagues back in 1964 with the San Francisco Giants, I was the first one-handed catcher in MLB history. It was a slog sometimes to convince my managers that it was the way to go. A lot of these guys were old school and cited the greats like Gabby Hartnett, Roy Campanella, and Mickey Cochrane—all two-handed catchers—as examples. They insisted that two-handed catching was far more effective when it came to blocking balls in the dirt and that with both hands on the mitt, the throwing hand is closer to the ball when it comes to cutting down a base-stealer.

I disagreed.

My argument was that with my throwing hand out of harm's way, I was able to be more effective (and healthy) for the season, not to mention that I had zero problem throwing runners out, be it second or third base. In my mind, my throwing arm was like a loaded weapon. As a catcher, keeping one eye on the base runner, and another eye on the pitcher, and also keeping track of the batter, is a mentally all-consuming process. No other position player has so much going on in every single play. I can remember how I felt when the great St. Louis Cardinal Lou Brock was perched on first base, with Ernie Banks holding him close, as Fergie, Nye, or Holtzman did their best to keep him on the base. But at some point, I knew Brock was going to take off, and when that happened, I needed everything in me to get the ball down to second base in time for Don Kessinger to try and tag him out.

A few years later the Cincinnati Reds catcher Johnny Bench adopted my style, and gradually it would become the standard way of playing behind the plate. Matter of fact, it's possible that Johnny picked up on my one-handed style while playing against the Cubs back in 1967, after getting nailed by a foul pitch on his throwing hand. Because of an odd setup in the season schedule that year, we played Cincinnati six out of the last seven regular-season games. I remember seeing this kid behind the plate, who was destined to become one of the great backstops of all time. Johnny was the complete package. It's also the first time that Johnny got to watch me up close from the opposing team's dugout, using only one hand, and when he returned for the 1968 season, he, too, had become a one-handed catcher!

The 1967 season was also the one in which I was awarded a Gold Glove, which honors the best defenders at each position. I led the league in put-outs, my fielding percentage behind the plate was .996, and I caught 152 games in a 162-game season. From 1967 to 1969 I caught 150+ games, and in 1968 I was behind the plate for a major league record of 160 games, the most games caught by a catcher in a season. This is a stat that I am so proud of and a record that still stands. Being behind the plate took a toll on my mind and body, and the only injury to my bare hand was when I busted my thumb on a play at the plate. But I never once broke a bone in my throwing hand from a foul tip thanks to my dad, who taught me to keep it out of harm's way.

****

Everything I achieved in my major league career began with that first mitt. You only can imagine how I felt when MacGregor came out with the 80-signature model catcher's mitt in 1968 with *my autograph* burned into the leather. In some ways, it was a serious full-circle moment. Imagine that, a hinged catcher's mitt, with my name on it, *which was being worn by catchers all over the country*, from kids on the sandlots to high school and college ballplayers.

My dad, Cecil Randolph Hundley Sr., passed away in 1988, at the age of 68. As I write this book and, recalling when he bought that mitt for me, so many seasons ago, I am moved to tears. My dad got to watch his son become one of the premiere catchers in baseball of my era, and it all started on that sunny afternoon, in our front yard, when he taught me to catch one-handed. It's not too much of a stretch to say that my dad, in so many ways, not only changed my life but also the game of baseball, as one-handed catching is now the only way to play the position.

1968 MacGregor 80 series autographed model

-2-
EARLY INNINGS

I'll never forget the moment when baseball fate came knocking.

It was February of 1958, I was in sociology class during my junior year, but as usual, I was thinking about baseball and all that goes along with it. I wasn't paying much attention to what was going on up on the blackboard when over the intercom at school came an announcement: *"Randolph Hundley, please report to the main office!"*

I didn't know what was up, but I was just glad I could get out of class.

There, standing in the principal's office, was a big man with a grin on his face.

"Hey, Randy! I'm Tim Murchison, a scout for the San Francisco Giants!" he announced as he stuck out his hand. "Great to meet you!"

I stood there, dumbfounded, and shook his hand, my heart seeming to race in my chest, and I could barely utter, "Nice to meet you, sir." I'd been on the radar of baseball scouts for a few months, but having one standing in front of me was a different story.

Tim Murchison had seen me playing American Legion ball between my sophomore and junior year when he'd been scouting older players, and I played well enough against the bigger guys to get his attention.

Tim started his baseball career back in 1917 as a 23-year-old southpaw, and he knocked around in the majors for a couple of years with both St. Louis and Cleveland. Like many players back then, he had racked up serious miles in semi-pro, and eventually his eye for talent landed him scouting jobs with various teams, and in 1953 he settled in with the San Francisco Giants. A few of the other players Tim brought to the big leagues during his career include catchers Rube Walker and Smoky Burgess, along with pitchers Gaylord Perry and Bobby Bolin, and third baseman Jim Ray Hart.

And now he was talking with me, in the principal's office at my high school.

After a short exchange, he gave me his business card with the Giants logo on it. I couldn't believe that he was interested in me and my abilities at the age of 17. With that card in my pocket, I went back to class and constantly checked it throughout the day to make sure that it was still there. A few times in class, I'd take it out and peek at it.

That night at the dinner table, my mom and dad were over-the-moon excited. We had a long conversation about what the future might hold and how to best move forward. Right then and there, my dad and I made an agreement. He would take on the role of coach, business director, PR guy, and agent. He would handle contract negotiations with any potential pro teams for me, and I would follow his lead, so I could keep my mind focused on playing baseball. We agreed that he would get 50% of any signing bonuses, which at that time had been limited to $4,000 before 1958. After some investigation, we thought I could land a bonus of $25,000. Big money back in the day!

As soon as I graduated from high school in 1960 (and thanks to Tim Murchison), the Giants

Signing day at the Hundley home

offered me a $110,000 bonus. It was to be paid out over five years because that's how long my dad figured it would take me to reach the majors. I would also be paid $1,000 per month during the baseball season. My dad's years in the construction business sure came in handy when it came to contracts and negotiations.

That amount of money was beyond my comprehension, and in today's money would be the equivalent of just over $1 million. The average signing bonus in MLB now is about $2.5 million and the average salary is $4.5 million. I was happy to get $1,000 a month! I was as rich as Rockefeller!

Oddly enough, I found out years later that there was some early interest in me from the Chicago Cubs, who decided to take a pass and signed an outfielder named Danny Murphy instead. Danny also signed a bonus-baby contract with the Cubs for $100,000 as an outfielder on June 15, 1960. Three days later, he made his professional and major league debut as the Cubs' starting center fielder in a game against the Cincinnati Reds at Crosley Field. He would become the youngest Cubs player to hit a home run at the age of 18 years and 3 weeks, when he hammered one out on September 13, 1960, off the Reds' Bob Purkey with two runners on base.

My first big purchase — a 1955 T-Bird!

****

My pro start came with Salem in the Class D Appalachian League when I turned 18 years old. The team was only about 50 miles from home, so I felt pretty good about things until I actually reported for camp. As it turned out, they didn't have any uniform pants that fit me, so I ended up wearing Tim Murchison's old uniform bottoms. There I was, about 5'11" and 160 pounds soaking wet, and Tim was a full 6'2" and easily weighed 100 pounds more than I did. All the other players on the team were waiting for me to show up, so they could check out the big money bonus baby. What they got wasn't a larger-than-life piece of granite, but rather a big-pants-wearing kid who looked completely out of place. But I dug in and made my presence known, even though on the inside I felt really intimidated.

On the second day of camp we were having an intrasquad game, and 90 feet down the line at third base was a former college football player, who was heading my way like a locomotive, trying to score on a single to left. This guy hit me like a ton of bricks, but I managed to stick my shin guard in his mid-section and hang on to the ball as he was called out at the plate. The skinny kid from Martinsville, the high-priced prospect who was wearing someone else's pants, made a statement on that first play at home. After that, my teammates saw me a little differently.

Then there was the time when our batting coach, the great Hank Sauer, pulled me aside for some instruction after my first few at-bats. Hank played in 1,399 games, mostly as a left fielder for the Reds, Cubs, Cardinals, and the New York/San Francisco Giants. He was a two-time All-Star and hit more than 30 home runs six times in the seven seasons of 1948 through 1954—including a career-high of 41 home runs in '54. Hank's best season came in 1952 when Sauer led the National League in home runs with 37 (tied with Ralph Kiner of the Pirates) and RBI (121) and was named the league MVP. Hank and Johnny Bench are the only players in MLB history ever to have hit three homers in a single game, twice against the same pitcher. Hank did it in 1950 and 1952 with the Cubs, both times off Curt Simmons of the Phillies.

So, when Hank Sauer offered up some pointers, I inhaled his baseball wisdom.

I had always twirled my bat prior to a pitch, for timing reasons. Hank called time out and said, "Randy, you are never going to hit big-league pitching like that." Hank taught me how to sit back on a pitch and determine what was coming my way. It took time for me to get used to a new stance, and because I had changed so much in such a short amount of time, when friends came to watch me in camp, they didn't even recognize me. It wasn't easy, but I was learning and growing from the high school phenom into a rookie ball player.

I spent the next two seasons with the Giants Class C affiliate team in Fresno, California. In 1962 my skills behind the plate made up for my .239 batting average, and I was bumped up to the El Paso Sun Kings in the Double-A Texas League, where my bat caught up with my catching. In 1963 I hit .325 with 23 home runs and 81 RBI at the age of 21. That El Paso team set a Texas record for home runs in a single season, and I made the Texas League All-Star team, leading the catchers in fielding as well. Even with all those stats, the Giants had a full cadre of catchers at that time and optioned me to the Minnesota Twins for one year. The Twins promptly sent me to their Triple-A level International League.

During the 1963 offseason, I was back home running a road grader and working construction with my dad when we heard on the radio that President Kennedy had been assassinated in Dallas. I will never forget the look of sadness frozen on my dad's face. Work ceased, and everything stood still as we absorbed the loss. I was early in my Christianity at that point and had a really hard time wondering how someone, *anyone*, could commit such an act. Sadly, it wouldn't be the last time I pondered such things, as the coming years would bring more of the same.

El Paso Sun Kings—1962

****

The long rocky road of minor league ball was exhausting and exhilarating at the same time. In many ways, I was king of the hill when I was in high school. Now I was playing with guys who were bigger, faster, and stronger, but I was still holding my own with them and honing my craft behind the plate. I had many phone calls with my dad over those early years. He would pump me up and help me keep my focus on the game, but if it hadn't been for Betty Foster, none of what I've accomplished would have been possible.

I knew who Betty was because we were both in the high school band, even though we never said anything more than an occasional "Good Morning." I played the clarinet and she played the saxophone. Our first date was set up after a basketball game when three of her friends were going out with their dates, and they asked her along. She needed to choose a date and she picked me. I was over-the-top flattered, but after our first "date," I cannot for the life of me figure out why she didn't move on. At that time (before the T-Bird) my car was a real beater, but I decided to be a big deal and drive everyone for this night out on the town. In short order, the muffler fell off, I got a flat tire, and Betty's dad had to rescue us, which surely wasn't the way to start a courtship.

Despite all of that, eventually, Betty became my high school sweetheart. She was a shining light, with a deep faith, and a smile that made me feel very special. After graduation, with me going into baseball and with Betty enrolling in a Bible college in North Carolina, we decided we would let things go for a year, but I missed her terribly. When she decided to go to college a second year, I was on my way to spring training in Arizona with Dick Dietz (who would go on to have an All-Star career as a catcher for the Giants.) Being away from Betty for so long was extremely difficult, especially since I knew the "Big Man on Campus" at her college was very interested in her. (I have to admit that whenever I played golf, I would envision his head as the golf ball, and boy did I have some incredible drives!) Sometimes I wondered if I would ever see her again. I tried to date a few times and eventually gave up on that because none of the girls measured up. I missed Betty, but I knew there wasn't much I could do about it. So, I offered it up to Christ in prayer and would allow the Lord to bring us together, if it was his will. Not long after, my prayers were answered.

Mr. & Mrs. Cecil Randolph Hundley Jr.

One day, out of the blue, Betty called and told me how much she missed me. We found each other again and eventually got married at the Tabernacle Baptist Church in Bassett, Virginia, on September 30, 1961. We were both so young, just 19 years old. Right after the wedding, we drove across the country to Arizona for winter ball. Those early innings, when Betty and I were building our lives together, are the most precious memories I have. Whenever I was on a road trip, I would count the days until I could be back home with her. We were young, in love, blessed, and on our way to the big leagues.

We went on to have four children in our family. Our oldest child is Julie, followed by Renee, then Todd (who played 15 years in the majors as a catcher, was a two-time All-Star with the Mets, the Dodgers, and also played two seasons with the Cubs), and finally Chad filled out the Hundley roster. While I have had some great success in baseball, what I am most proud of is my family.

Even though she was my biggest cheerleader, Betty never really cared much about going to the games, but rather she enjoyed being at home and taking care of our children as they grew up. She was an incredible wife and mother. Just knowing I would go home to Betty and she would have dinner waiting for me at the end of the day gave me a great sense of peace, which allowed me to concentrate on calling pitches, arguing with umps, and throwing out potential base-stealers. She was my rock, my best friend, and my partner, and was always there with the right words no matter what was going on. Betty's presence over my years in and out of the game was formidable and her support in so many ways was the building blocks of my many steps on the baseball path. I had someone who totally supported me, and that made all the difference in my growing confidence, on and off the field.

I finally made my major league debut with the Giants on September 27, 1964, not behind the plate, but as a pinch-runner

First game at Wrigley

for the great Duke Snider, and at Wrigley Field of all places. Our opponent was the team that I would eventually be traded to, the Chicago Cubs, who won the game 4–2.

****

In 1965, I began to split time between Triple-A Tacoma and the Giants until their regular catcher, Tom Haller, got injured and I was called up to take his place. It became my job to try and throw out the lightning-quick Maury Wills, who was a speed demon on the base path. The first two games I played were back-to-back night games against the rival LA Dodgers, and I had to face the intimidating Don Drysdale first, and then the legendary Sandy Koufax in the second game.

There I was, just 24 years old on June 28, 1965, with the fiery Drysdale staring me down from the mound. He had a reputation for putting batters on their backs with the inside heat. I was new meat, and sure enough, the first time I faced Don he yelled, "LOOK OUT!" as he promptly threw the first pitch at my head. This had my fanny in the dirt and then Dodger catcher John Roseboro smiled and said, "Welcome to the big leagues, kid." I got up, knocked the dirt off my uniform, got back in the box, and promptly fouled off the next two pitches, which was an accomplishment in and of itself. But as a bit of payback in the 2nd inning, Roseboro popped a ball straight up over home plate and I tossed my mask away, camped out under it, and caught it to retire the side. In the 5th inning, I pushed a bunt toward the mound, which Drysdale muffed, and Hal Lanier scored from third. I think that bunt was my first RBI in MLB. We won that game, 5–0.

In the second game at Candlestick Park, I went 0–2 at the plate against Koufax who was nicknamed "The Left Arm of God." He had a rising fastball and a curve that started at the top of your head and would drop so fast it would buckle your knees. After he threw me that looping curve ball for the third time, I swung and got nothing but air. I stepped out of the batter's box, put some dirt on my hands, and said to the Dodger catcher, *"Mr. Roseboro, I've got to find a brown paper bag, pack a lunch, and get a real job because I am flat overmatched here."*

It's easy to sit home and watch a game, yelling when a batter strikes out, but I'm here to tell you, hitting a round ball that's coming at you upward of 90 miles per hour, or hitting the hanging curve in the just the right spot on a round baseball bat is a matter of athletic timing, physics, and a little bit of luck.

Even though I enjoyed my time in San Francisco, it was obvious that I was stuck in neutral. Herman Franks, the Giants manager, still thought that catching one-handed wasn't the way to go, and I'm sure that kept me out of a lot of games. Betty and I had many conversations about my anxiety about being in that position, so finally, after six years, I gave the Giants an ultimatum: "Play me, replace me, or trade me." This was the right thing to do but was difficult because of my loyalty to the organization and mostly because of Tim Murchison and the opportunity he gave me when I was just a teenager with dreams of big-league ball.

Not long after the 1965 season wrapped up, on December 2nd, pitcher Bill Hands and I were traded to the Chicago Cubs for pitcher Lindy McDaniel and outfielder Don Landrum.

The Cubs had finished in eighth place in 1965, and the organization decided it was time for a major overhaul, which included hiring Leo "the Lip" Durocher as manager. He promptly declared that the Cubs were a far better team than their record. Durocher had played shortstop on two winning World Series teams—the 1928 Yankees and the 1934 Cardinals. He also coached the Giants to victory in the 1954 World Series and is the guy who coined the phrase "nice guys finish last," which is all you need to know about Leo's communication and leadership style. He was loud and over the top, a looming figure in both baseball and with his pals in Hollywood.

On the topic of the trade, Leo was quoted as saying, "We got a young kid who can throw the ball and is the best catching prospect in a Cubs uniform since Gabby Hartnett." Charles "Gabby" Hartnett played for the Cubs from 1922 to 1940 and is considered the greatest catcher in MLB history (ranked alongside Johnny Bench). He is famous for his "Homer in the Gloamin'," when, with one week left in the 1938 season, he hit a game-winning home run in the bottom of the 9th inning to put the Cubs in first place. Gabby cranked out the homer as darkness enveloped Wrigley Field, making it nearly impossible to see the ball. At the time of his retirement, Hartnett held the career records for catchers in home runs, runs batted in, hits, doubles, and most games played as a catcher. Gabby Hartnett was inducted into the Baseball Hall of Fame in 1955.

However, Durocher's admiration for me didn't last long.

Three or four days into spring training before the 1966 season, Leo called a clubhouse meeting and slowly went around the room, taking digs at each player, first getting on the legendary Charlie Grimm. *"I don't want to see your face in my dugout any-more."* Charlie played for the Pirates early in his career but was traded to the Cubs in 1925 and worked mostly for the Cubs for the rest of his career. His 946 wins as a Cubs manager rank second behind the great Cap Anson. Charlie was one of the most beloved Cubs of all time and Leo's remarks hurt him deeply. Leo continued hammering guys one by one, including "Mr. Cub" Ernie Banks, telling him in no uncertain terms that he wanted Ernie to tag the runner on first, no matter how many times the pitcher threw over to keep them close to the bag. Leo cursed out Ernie like he was a rookie. He moved through the locker room and no one was spared, not even our clubhouse manager, Yosh Kawano, who never bothered anyone. Leo barked, *"Listen you little Jap. You do exactly what I tell you to do, nothing more, nothing less."* One by one he lowered the boom on his players, myself included: *"Hundley, if you can't cut it behind the plate, I will find someone who will."* He scared the crap outta me. I guess he was trying to motivate us, but in those moments it seemed more like a father scolding his children than a professional baseball manager trying to rally his troops.

Matter of fact, while it took me a couple of years to see it, there were many similarities between Leo Durocher and my dad. Their intense, no-nonsense approach to the game and willingness to use a big stick if needed made it an easy comparison.

Even so, the nucleus of the team was beginning to form with Ernie Banks, Glenn Beckert, Don Kessinger, Ron Santo, Billy Williams, and myself in the lineup. Ferguson Jenkins, Ken Holtzman, Rich Nye, Ted Abernathy, and Bill Hands were all part of the pitching rotation. Other players like Paul Popovich, Adolfo Phillips, Joey Amalfitano, and Byron Brown filled out the roster. A couple of big guys, 6' 5" Don Bryant and 6' 4" Chris Krug, were the backup catchers behind me. Yosh Kawano gave me #9 to wear, the number that Hank Sauer made famous for the Cubs as the league MVP in 1952, and that Javi Baez would also wear many years later in the 2016 World Series.

I had a tremendous year with 1966 as my first full rookie season. The 149 games I caught that year set a National League record, and I also finished third among catchers in home runs. In May, just two months into the season, I had a fantastic game against the Houston Astros, hitting a double, a triple, and even stealing home in a 7–1 rout. One month later I hit my first major league grand slam, which is always a big deal, but was a *really big deal* for me because I got another chance for payback. It was Don

My first year in Cubs pinstripes—1966

Drysdale who served up a fastball that I hit right on the screws, a serious rocket that left the park in a hurry. I couldn't help but trot around the bases with a big smile on my face, but not *too* big. I didn't want to make Drysdale mad because I would pay for it in my next at-bat for sure. Later in the summer, we were back in Houston, and I hit for the cycle on August 11th in a 9–8, 11-inning victory against the Astros. I set a major league record that season with the most home runs by a rookie catcher with 19 round-trippers. I tied for fourth place in the voting for the Rookie of the Year Award that was won by Tommy Helms of the Reds.

Unfortunately, we lost 103 games and finished in 10th place. A record worse than the 1965 team, and much of that was due to the fact we were trying to come together as a ball club and figure out exactly what Durocher was demanding from us to become winners. While I was glad to be on the Cubs and playing every day, Leo was a madman compared to Herman Franks. His caustic managerial style had our heads spinning and his constant berating of players, coaches, and anyone within earshot was overwhelming, to say the least.

Most days Leo pushed me like a plow horse. One time he was trying to get my attention from the dugout. He started screaming my name and jumping up and down, and in doing so, hit his head on the dugout roof. He sat there the rest of the game bleeding down his neck. After the game, I saw him in the locker room getting stitches in his bald head. He didn't jump up much after that. He pushed every button I had, and even the ones I didn't know existed. Leo Durocher flat wore me out.

There were many times Betty talked me off the ledge, and just knowing I had her in my corner made all the difference. I'd come home after another loss, or a chewing-out from Durocher, and think to myself, *if this is what major league baseball is about, I don't want any part of it.* Through it all Betty was steadfast, and her strength and faith helped to prop me up even when I didn't think the game was worth it.

We got pretty beat up that year, on and off the field. I took that winter to rest up, and my offseason was spent building out my "Randy's Family Hobby Center" back in Collinsville, Virginia. The hobby center helped me to keep my mind off baseball for the time being. Truth be told, another season with Leo in my ear and riding my fanny wasn't something I looked forward to, and if it was going to be a repeat of the '66 season, I was thinking that the hobby car model business would be a better career for me. Hanging up the cleats and mask might not be such a bad idea in the long run.

But it wasn't all bad.

As I look at this Topps All-Star Rookie Team card from back in 1966, I remember why I had such a big smile on my face. It wasn't just because I was on my way to becoming an established catcher, it was because standing just behind the photographer, Willie Mays, Orlando Cepeda, and Willie McCovey were making faces at me so I would crack up.

Imagine that, three future Hall of Famers goofing off just to make me smile. It worked then, and all these years later, it still does.

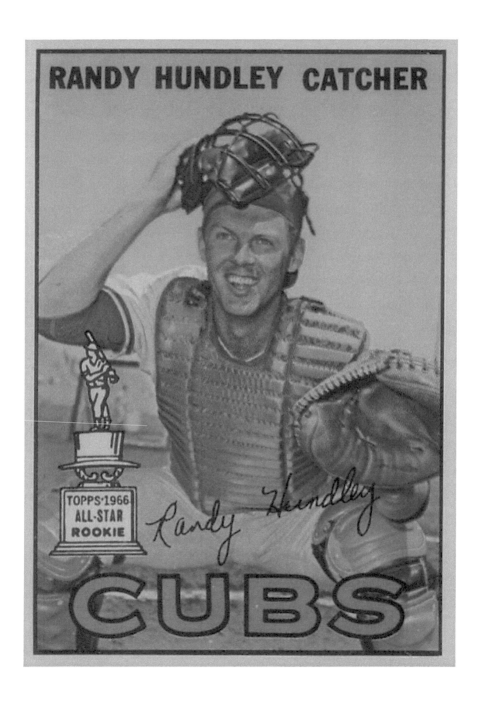

-3-
THE REBEL

Not long after I arrived in Chicago, it was pretty obvious to my teammates that I wasn't a native of the Windy City, as my Southern drawl points to Dixieland roots. My hometown of Martinsville, Virginia, was part of the Confederacy during the Civil War. One of the last battles of the war took place in Martinsville on April 8, 1865, when Union Colonel William J. Palmer's brigade under General George Stoneman's command marched through Henry County, the very place where I grew up. The next day, April 9, 1865, Confederate General Robert E. Lee surrendered to Union General Ulysses S. Grant at the Appomattox Court House, effectively ending the Civil War. Northern pro-Union supporters considered the Civil War as the "War of Rebellion" and dubbed the Confederate supporters and soldiers as "Rebels." And, to think that 100 years after the Civil War ended (almost to the day) I was playing pro baseball, amazes me.

From 1959 to 1961, the same years I was breaking into baseball, there was a popular television series starring Nick Adams as the titular character in *Johnny Yuma*: a displaced Confederate soldier haunted by his memories of the Civil War, wandering from one adventure to another. The theme song of the show was sung by Johnny Cash and was called "The Rebel—Johnny Yuma" after the main title of the show.

It didn't take long for someone in the Chicago Cubs clubhouse to connect my Virginia drawl with that song and now and then, I could hear the boys in the clubhouse singing the alternative lyrics to the Cash song: *"Randy Hundley was a rebel, he roamed through the West…"* Somehow the fans picked up on it, and from that point on I was "The Rebel" and joined the ranks of some of the Chicago Cubs greatest nicknames.

Of course, "Mr. Cub" Ernie Banks tops the list. Then you have pitcher Mordecai Brown, who was called "Three Fingers" because he lost two digits in a farm machinery accident. "Sweet Swinging" Billy Williams was in homage to Billy's flawless arc from the left-handed side of the plate. The great Cubs second baseman from back in the early 1900s Johnny Evers was part of the famous "Tinkers to Evers to Chance" line in the poem entitled "Baseball's Sad Lexicon." His nickname was "The Human Crab," which described the way he would move to scoop up ground balls, plus he had a really short temper, which I can relate to. Add to the list some other great Cubs nicknames like Dave "Kong" Kingman, "The Red Baron" Rick Sutcliffe, "Mad Dog" Greg Maddux, and "The Penguin" Ron Cey, as well as my old battery mate Bill "Froggy" Hands, and you have quite the cast of characters.

Baseball can be a frustrating game at times, and the language used on and off the field is often coarse with a stream of curse words (usually toward an umpire) that is used to underscore a disagreed call or play. Leo Durocher was a master at this, spewing out curse words in such rapid-fire succession that he made swearing an art form. When I was a kid growing up, I fell in line with the language on the playground, but when I became a born-again Christian in my teens, I ditched the foul language. Oddly enough, in some ways, I was more known for *not swearing* because it was just as effective to say, "What the crap!" to an ump who missed a strike call, or to tell someone to "kiss my hillbilly fanny" to get my point across. So, while I was given the nickname "The Rebel," I wanted to maintain my status in the game as a hardnosed catcher who didn't need to drop F-bombs to make my case. I would leave that up to Durocher, who had more than enough to go around. I cannot imagine what Leo would say if he was mic'd up like some of the managers are today.

****

Coming out of the dismal 1966 season, I was looking forward to 1967, but my optimism didn't last long. During a spring training game, I injured my left knee and ankle and missed the first three regular-season games against the Phillies that year. It killed me not to be ready for Opening Day, as Fergie Jenkins would be on the mound. Dick Bertell filled in for me behind the plate and did a great job catching Jenkins and then Ken Holtzman in the second game of the season. Then, we had our first road-trip game to Forbes Field to play the Pirates, and John Boccabella was behind the dish to catch the starter, Curt Simmons. On Saturday, April 15th, I was finally good to go, and with Ray Culp on the mound, I would stay in my crouch from that point on, catching in every game through June. Playing the Pirates was always a battle, as they had the great Roberto Clemente, slugger Willie Stargell, Matty Alou, speedy Maury Wills, and Bill Mazeroski in their daily lineup at that time.

Tough guys and a tough team, but we were starting to come into our own as a ball club, and we knew playing teams that, on paper, looked stronger just made us that much more determined to win, and win we did. We took two out of three games in that early season series against the Pirates.

Then on June 19th, I got the news that I was hoping for. Back in spring training, I had to take two days off of camp, and I spent six hours in a courtroom trying to convince a judge that the IRS was dead wrong in not allowing me to declare the money I paid my dad from my first contract with the Giants in 1960 as a business expense on my taxes. My dad acted as my coach and I paid him as such, but that didn't sit well with the IRS, who responded with a lawsuit claiming it was an "unallowable expense." When we got to the courtroom my dad said, "Son, just let this go. I don't want to make this more difficult for you." I said, "Daddy, we didn't do anything wrong, and I am going to see this through to the end." I had forgotten my mitt at the hotel and was going to make the case that my dad was my coach without it, but my lawyer insisted I go back and get it. In the end, the judge boiled a long legal diatribe down to this: "The only question presented for our decision is what portion of a $22,000 cash bonus earned by the petitioner in 1960 for signing a professional baseball contract is deductible as the reasonable value of services actually performed by petitioner's father." This went back and forth for most of the day, and I was asked more than a couple of times to demonstrate the one-handed catching technique my dad taught me, to validate my demand for the business expense. Every time I squatted down in that hot courtroom, I kept thinking how ridiculous the whole thing was. In the end, the judge ruled in our favor: "We hold, therefore, that whereas the respondent acted correctly in including the entire $22,000 bonus in the petitioner's taxable income, the petitioner should be nevertheless allowed a deduction in the amount of $11,000 in 1960 as a business expense for the portion of the bonus paid directly to Cecil Randolph Hundley Sr. for his personal services actually rendered with such rewarding financial results for both the petitioner and his father."

The next day newspapers around the country ran a story about the IRS thing with the title "Hundley Beats Rap." I've always wondered if the judge was a Cubs fan.

****

By July 2nd, we were tied for the National League lead with the St. Louis Cardinals, as we both had 46–29 records. By that point in the season, I had caught 74 games in a row, as well as both ends of nine doubleheaders. Our bats had come alive in a big way, and we had racked up 370 runs and allowed 292.

On July 3rd, we had a serious day at the plate, as we battled the Atlanta Braves.

The Braves had Tony Cloninger on the mound, with the one and only Bob Uecker behind the plate. Paul Popovich and Glenn Beckert both got on base to start the game, and then Billy Williams came to the plate and proceeded to park the first pitch into the right-field seats with a three-run dinger. Ron Santo stepped in next and launched one out of the park, making the score 4–0 and managing to knock Cloninger out of the game in the 1st inning. The Braves put Dick Kelley on the mound and

Al Spangler grabbed a walk, which put me in the batter's box. Kelley grooved a fastball right in my wheelhouse, and as a pull-hitter, I hammered the ball deep into the cheap seats in left field at Atlanta Fulton-County Stadium.

We were up 6–0 in the 1st inning.

Ray Culp was on the mound, a big strong right-hander, who had some serious steam on the ball when needed. As a rookie, Ray made the 1963 NL All-Star team and went on to retire Al Kaline, Frank Malzone, and Carl Yastrzemski in order. No easy feat. But he'd have his work cut out for him because the Braves had some serious lumber in their lineup, including Hank Aaron, Rico Carty, and Clete Boyer.

The Braves lead-off man was Felipe Alou, the first player from the Dominican Republic to play regularly in the big leagues and the most well-known and prominent member of one the most notable families in baseball history. He is the oldest of the trio of baseball-playing brothers that included Matty and Jesús, who were both primarily outfielders, and his son Moisés was also an outfielder; and all but Jesús have been named All-Stars at least twice.

Felipe was a hard-slugging first baseman for the Braves and I knew he had power, so I had Culp throw him an off-speed pitch, just to try and soften him up and slow him down, but Alou caught the ball square on the sweet spot and it sailed off his bat, deep into the left field seats. We got the next two batters, and then Rico Carty stepped in and proceeded to drill a pitch into nearly the same spot that Alou did, into deep left. Then it was 6–2, and we finally got out of the inning as Clete Boyer grounded out to Santo at third.

The game stayed that score until the top of the 6th when I hit a single into center field. I moved to second on a sacrifice bunt from Culp, but the throw at first was muffed by Alou, and then we had two of us on the bags. Up came Glenn Beckert, who wasn't known for having much power, but that didn't matter, as he hit the first pitch off middle reliever Jay Ritchie into the left field seats, and then we were up 9–2.

But the Braves weren't quite done. "Hammerin' Hank" Aaron hit a sharp line drive to left field, putting him at first base, followed by Carty, who hammered one of his own out of the park, and then it was 9–4.

The 7th inning was where the game got really wild in Atlanta.

Clay Carroll was on the mound for the Braves. Lee Thomas, who was playing first base for us that game, got a single. Al Spangler followed with a ball in the gap, just out of the reach of Aaron, which pushed Thomas to third and put Spangler on second base with a double. I was up next and hit a ball right off the tip of my bat, a dribbler back to the mound. Carroll charged the ball and barely got me out on the play to first, but it also kept the runners in check. They walked our center-fielder Ted Savage intentionally to load the bases to get to Ray Culp, but Leo pulled him and put in backup catcher John Stephenson to pinch-hit. Stephenson then proceeded to push a ball deep into center field and out of the reach of Mack Jones. The bases cleared as Thomas and Spangler scored, and Savage made it home from first base.

The Cubs won 12–6, and it is a game that stands out in my memory for a couple of reasons. Those five home runs in the 1st inning tied the record for round-trippers at that time. It was really something to watch the ball sail out of the park in such a rapid-fire way. Secondly, being on the same field with Henry Aaron was always a big deal for me, as I appreciated and respected his place in the game. Also, there was no way to know back then that Bob Uecker would become a cultural icon when Johnny Carson called him "Mr. Baseball." Not bad for a guy with a career .200 batting average, but he did hit a homer off Koufax, so you gotta give him that. Later in 1967, Uecker was traded to the Phillies in exchange for catcher Gene Oliver, who would become a close friend to me for many years.

****

By the time of the All-Star break in '67, I had caught every inning of 78 games and was holding a .300 batting average, which is difficult to do, as the strain behind the plate takes a toll on catchers, more than any other position in baseball. By this time, Leo had softened on me a bit, and one day pulled me aside and said, "Randy, I'm turning the on-field game over to you, you're the manager out there, and whatever you say, goes."

At first, I didn't know exactly what to think, but somehow Durocher's reverse psychology had the desired effect on me. In many ways, I'd been preparing for this role ever since I squatted down in the front yard in Martinsville to play catch with my dad. Leo's confidence in me gave me the leadership role that was needed for the club at the time, and I accepted it with great responsibility. In some ways, his hard-nosed ways had rubbed off on me, pushing my "take no crap" attitude to the next level. You can't be a creampuff behind the plate.

I was having such a fantastic year that a Chicago sportswriter named Jerome Holtzman (no relation to Kenny) said that I should get the MVP award from the Cubs right then and there. "He is probably the finest defensive catcher in the league," Holtzman wrote. "Moreover, he is now learning how to take charge of a game and is handling the Cubs staff with the poise of an established veteran." Shucks, I was just a 25-year-old kid playing the game I loved, but it was an honor to be considered the same caliber as other catchers like Tim McCarver of the Cardinals, my former Giants teammate Tom Haller, John Roseboro of the Dodgers, and that guy over in Cincinnati, Johnny Bench.

As we began to win more games, the fans started to return to Wrigley Field. The attendance numbers were dismal in 1966. Pitcher Rich Nye said the paid attendance was 405 at one game and there were more vendors than fans in the ballpark. While the average was about 7,500 fans for home games, it wasn't unusual to see only 1,500 people at the ballpark. In 1967, we began to average about 12,800 fans per game, because winning always is the best way to increase ticket sales. By 1969, that number had more than doubled to just over 25,000 fans who showed up at "The Friendly Confines" on a regular basis. Back then, general admission was priced at $1.50 per ticket; box seats were going for around $3.50 each. I can remember pulling up to the ballpark and seeing long lines of fans waiting to get into the bleachers. For $1, you could park your backside on the long, wooden green-painted planks in the outfield. In those days, you could just stay for a doubleheader, at no extra charge.

****

For me, 1967 is the season I turned a corner in my major league career. I was getting more and more comfortable calling games from behind the plate. The pitchers trusted me to get them through tough innings by knowing the tendencies of the opposing batters. At the plate, I found my groove and finished with a respectable .267 batting average. Mentally I was getting tougher, even though my body took a pounding. I established a major league record for the fewest errors by a catcher in 150 or more games and broke the NL mark for fewest passed balls in 150 or more games. I was tied with Bob Gibson, Tom Seaver, and Jim Bunning (all future Hall of Famers) in the MVP voting, which was won by Orlando Cepeda that year; Ron Santo came in 4th. Due to my work behind the plate, I made the NL MVP roster and I was awarded a Gold Glove for my efforts. Since 1957, the Gold Glove honors the best defenders at each position in each league, and in 1986 Jody Davis became the only other Chicago Cubs catcher to win a Gold Glove in club history. I cannot accurately find the words to share with you how proud my dad was that I earned that Gold Glove. The man who taught me everything about catching deserved it as much as I did. All his hard work paid off, both on the field and in the courtroom, as captured by the famous sports cartoonist, the late Murray Olderman.

That 1967 season didn't go exactly as planned by Durocher, but we finished a respectable 3rd place, 10½ games behind the Giants, and a full 14 games behind the tough St. Louis Cardinals, who would go on to win the World Series that year, defeating the Boston Red Sox 4 games to 3. We had moved up from 10th place to 3rd, with an 87–74 W/L record, and the team was really starting to find its chemistry under the constant pounding from Durocher, who was whipping us into shape, both physically and mentally. There is no doubt that Leo was a taskmaster, and some writers have called him the baseball equivalent of the great football coach Vince Lombardi, who was also known for being relentless, as he built the Green Bay Packers from one of the worst teams in the NFL to one of the best, winning five championships as well as Super Bowls I and II.

The progress we had made since the 1966 season had my spirits up a bit, and while there was no let-up on Leo's part, I felt better about going into the offseason than I had at any other time in my career up to that point. The next year, 1968, would prove to be a major push forward, not only for me but also the Chicago Cubs, as we were starting to put the puzzle pieces together and becoming a force to be reckoned with on the diamond.

-4-
SUMMER OF CHANGE

In 1968, the pressure was on us in a big way. Previously the Cubs had just one winning season from 1947 to 1966, so after the much-improved 1967 season, we had some work to do in order to prove that we weren't a fluke. That year there were five catchers on the roster. I was in the starting position behind the plate with backup from Randy Bobb, John Boccabella, John Felske, and Bill Plummer, who rode the bench most of the season. But to show how things can change in baseball, one year later, in January of 1969, Plummer was traded from the Cubs to the Reds for pitcher Ted Abernathy (who previously played for the Cubs '65–'66 and then was traded to the Braves and the Reds before returning), and Bill eventually worked himself into the regular slot backing up Johnny Bench for seven seasons. Abernathy became a submarine-style pitcher after having torn two shoulder muscles in his freshman year of high school, and to overcome the injury he learned to throw to home plate by releasing the ball just inches from the ground, which is the opposite of most pitchers who come from the overhand release. Catching Ted with that unorthodox delivery was challenging, to say the least, and it took more than a little getting used to. While Abernathy only played one more season with the Cubs, he had a good career and led the National League in games pitched three times: 1965 (with 84, a major league record at the time), 1967, and 1968.

For the most part, the team had gotten used to Leo's rants, and he continued pressuring us to keep improving. He didn't ride my backside as much as he did in the first couple of seasons, but it was obvious that Durocher also had his back against the wall and he started using some interesting tactics to get us to move our butts on the field. Sometimes it worked; other times it didn't. I can remember when we played our first games in the Houston Astrodome, in May of 1966. Durocher was an old-school manager and playing in a dome was, as he put it, "A $45 million stadium with a 10-cent infield." He hated the concept of "AstroTurf" and thought it was made of nylon (even though there was still some real grass in the outfield). We got swept in that first series and outscored 18–5 over three games. Our second trip to Houston in the middle of the season had us losing again, and this time Leo took his frustrations out on the phone in the dugout by ripping it off the wall! The Cubs had to pay for the replacement phone.

But he wasn't done yet.

Our final trip to the Astrodome was in August, and we were 44–82 at that point and over 30 games out of first place. In the first game of that series, we took a 4–1 lead into the bottom of the 9th inning with Ken Holtzman having a really good game on the mound. John Bateman led off the inning for Houston with a homer to make it 4–2. Holtzman then allowed a single and walk, and Durocher came out to replace him. The big scoreboard in the Astrodome showed a cartoon animation of a Cubs player taking a shower with his fanny hanging out, a reference to the fact the Holtzman was done for the day. While reliever Bob Hendley was making his warm-up throws, Leo promptly went back to the dugout, tore the phone off the wall again, and this time threw it out onto the playing field! I can remember seeing the thing fly out of the dugout and thinking, *"What the crap?"*

Leo was fuming and the Astros knew it.

To make matters worse, Hendley walked Joe Morgan to load the bases, then gave up an infield single that made it 4–3 Cubs. To cap off the inning, Bob Aspromonte hit a walk-off grand slam for a 7–4 Houston win. I thought Durocher was going to have a heart attack right there on the spot.

Ironically, Leo Durocher would finish his coaching career with the Houston Astros, for one season '72 from '73. Rumor had it that the Astros put extra bolts in the dugout phones to make sure they stayed on the wall while Leo was manager. As a side note, during the time the Cubs played in the Astrodome, we had little success there, going 83–137 from 1965 to 1999, by far our worst record in any park outside Wrigley Field during those years.

****

Ernie Banks had long been the face of the club by the time I joined the team. In addition to being called "Mr. Cub," he was also known as "Mr. Sunshine" because of his outlook on life. So, when Ernie smiled broadly and said, *"The Cubs will be great in '68!"* he meant it. And we believed it. We were starting to crawl out of the standings cellar, and the team that had played so well in '67 was pretty much intact.

The infield was made up of Banks at first (14x All-Star and the league MVP in '58 and '59 and Gold Glove winner in '60.) Rock-solid infielder Glenn Beckert (4x All-Star and a Gold Glove winner in '68) at second base, rangy Don Kessinger at short-stop (Gold Glove in '69 and '70 and 6x All-Star), perennial Gold Glove–winner Ron Santo (and 9x All-Star) at third, and I was behind the plate, coming off my best year in the majors up to that point. The pitching ranks still had Fergie Jenkins as our ace, plus Bill Hands, Ken Holtzman, Rich Nye, Joe Niekro, "The Vulture" Phil Reagan, and rounding out a lineup of great arms were Chuck Hartenstine, Jack Lamabe, and Archie Reynolds. The outfield had "Gentleman" Jim Hickman in right, speedy Adolfo Phillips in center, and Billy Williams (Rookie of the Year in '61 and 6x All-Star) in left. Al Spangler, Willie Smith, and Lou Johnson, along with Jimmy McMath, filled in as needed, as did Gene Oliver (who was acquired from the Red Sox in June of '68), Dick Nen, and future Cubs manager Lee Elia who was the Cubs skipper from '82 to '83. Lee is now known for his profanity-filled tirade, targeting the fans (or lack of them) at Wrigley at a press conference after a 4–3 loss to the Dodgers, with only 9,300 fans in the stands in April of '83. Lee was a scrappy ballplayer, to say the least, and there are just times the game gets to a fella, especially if you are the manager. Unfortunately, there were microphones on, and the "Elia Rant" will live on forever because of that recording. I wonder what Lee would have thought about having fewer than 500 fans in the stands, as we often did in 1966.

While baseball is a fairly simple game, assembling the right pieces that create success takes time, and there needs to be chemistry for the machine to run at peak performance. We had the right guys in the right positions to pick up where we left off and to make a serious playoff run against our arch-rivals, the St. Louis

Cardinals who won the World Series in 1967, as well as the usual scheduled teams in the National League: the Reds, Pirates, Braves, Mets, Phillies, Giants, Astros, and Dodgers. It wasn't until 1969 that East/West divisions were created, with the addition of the San Diego Padres and Montreal Expos for the NL and Seattle Pilots (later to become the Milwaukee Brewers) and the Kansas City Royals to the AL. But some other things were going on in 1968 that made it a difficult year, and it was often hard to concentrate on baseball because the headlines were busy, and much of it wasn't good.

****

The Vietnam War was raging, and in January of '68, North Vietnam launched the Tet Offensive against the United States and South Vietnam. The coordinated attack by 85,000 Viet Cong and North Vietnamese targeted 36 major cities and towns in South Vietnam. It caught US-led forces by surprise. It was the beginning of a major shift when it came to support for the war, and the unrest and turmoil in America were starting to simmer and would eventually boil over.

On April 4th, we were in Evansville, Indiana, for an exhibition game, just a few days before our season opener against the Cincinnati Reds on the 10th. I can remember Fergie running down the hallway of our hotel like a man on fire. When I asked him what was wrong he said, "Martin Luther King Jr. was gunned down in Memphis, and I am locking myself in my hotel room." Not long after, I ran into Billy Williams and tried to express my deep sorrow. Billy said, *"Randy, this is what we deal with all the time."* It pierced my heart to hear my friend say those words. They canceled the exhibition game, and I can remember watching this tragedy unfold and wondering what the heck was happening in our country. It didn't take long for violence to break out in response to King's assassination, and Chicago had more than 48 hours of rioting that would leave 11 dead and 48 wounded. Mayor Daley issued a "shoot-to-kill" order, and parts of the city were burned to the ground.

I was glad that we were heading out on a road trip, even though every major city experienced some sort of rioting after the King assassination. By the time we opened at Wrigley on April 13th, things had quieted down a bit, but you could feel the tension in the air. We won 8 games and lost 10 in April, and in some respects, baseball just didn't seem that important when compared to so much of what was going on around the game. I did my best to keep what was going on outside of the game tucked away, but it wasn't easy. We all felt it.

Even though I grew up in Virginia, which was part of the Confederacy just over a century earlier, I never understood the racist views of the South. When I started playing ball on traveling teams, my teammates and opposing players were often mixed-race. For me, baseball was the great equalizer, and no one cared what color your skin was, or where you came from. What mattered was if you could play the game, contribute, and perform on the field. There were many road trips where some of my teammates had to use segregated restaurants, hotels, and washrooms. Here we were, playing and traveling together as a team, and when we'd stop in a Southern city to play, my teammates of color had to go a different route. It made no sense to me at all. The same guys who were being cheered on during the game were made to feel like second-class citizens after it was over. Even when a teammate was called up to the big leagues, they often still had to put up with segregation and racism.

In 1953 Ernie Banks became the first Black player ever drafted by the Chicago Cubs. He was fresh off a stint in the US Army after being stationed in Germany during the Korean War. Ernie lettered in football, baseball, and track in high school and eventually became a member of the Amarillo Colts, a semi-professional baseball team. Ernie never played in the minors and made his major league debut at Wrigley Field at the age of 22. He was well aware of the racial divide in baseball, and during his first game for the Cubs, Banks received a visit from the great Jackie Robinson that influenced his quiet presence in baseball. Robinson reportedly said, "Ernie, I'm glad to see you're up here, so now just listen and learn ..." A few years later when Ernie thought about speaking up a bit, he discussed it with Billy Williams, who advised him to let his play on the field do the talking. Ernie said, "I kept my mouth shut, but tried to make a difference. My whole life, I've just wanted to make people better."

Ernie's views on that time in our nation's history were straightforward.

"My philosophy about race relations is that I'm the man and I'll set my own patterns in life. I don't rely on anyone else's opinions. I look at a man as a human being; I don't care about his color. Some people feel that because you are Black you will never be treated fairly and that you should voice your opinions and be militant about them. I don't feel this way. You can't convince a fool against his will . . . If a man doesn't like me because I'm Black, that's fine. I'll just go elsewhere, but I'm not going to let him change my life."

For the record, none of us who wore the Cubs pinstripes, and played during the years Ernie Banks was on the team, ever saw him as anything other than a legendary ballplayer. He was a leader in every sense of the word and every bit as important to the game as Jackie Robinson was, in terms of being a quiet example of a great human being both on and off the field.

****

We were facing the New York Mets on June 5th at Wrigley. The Mets had Tom Seaver on the mound and we had Rich Nye throwing for us. It was an afternoon game, usually with a 1:20 p.m. start, and there were around 6,400 fans in the stands, on a bright and warm summer afternoon. At that point, the Mets were 22–27 and we were 25–22 and holding steady because of a pretty good start to the season. In this game, Banks hit a double, triple, and jacked his 9th homer of the year. Williams, Phillips, and Johnson hit triples, and Beckert and Phillips both hit doubles. I went one for three with two walks and a single. The Mets were attempting to steal bases like they were made of gold, but I shot down Agee and Cleon Jones in order. But we came up short, losing the game 4–2.

That night I was at home with Betty, who was taking care of my aches and pains and keeping me well fed so my weight stayed up. After a good night's sleep, I woke up to the news that Robert F. Kennedy had been shot at a presidential campaign rally in Los Angeles. He was in critical condition, and his last words from the podium were, "So my thanks to all of you, and on to Chicago, and let's win there." My heart sank because I couldn't hardly believe it. First, Martin Luther King Jr. and just a couple of months later, Bobby Kennedy. It seemed at times like the world was falling apart, and perhaps it was, but we still had a game to play, as the world waited to learn the fate of the 42-year-old Kennedy.

On June 6th, the Mets had Dick Selma (who would join the Cubs in 1969) on the mound, and we had Kenny Holtzman throwing for us. Santo knocked his 9th homer of the year, Ernie had a double, and Kessinger added a triple, but the Mets lineup cranked it up with two homers from Ed Charles and Ron Swaboda, and Tommie Agee tripled, and this time both Agee and Cleon Jones stole second base on Kenny and me. We lost the game 5–3 in front of 5,858 fans at Wrigley, as both teams seemed somewhat distracted: the summer of '68 was becoming more and more volatile by the day. The nation was battered and fatigued, a feeling I understand on the physical level.

Since he'd been shot, millions had held their breath, only to learn that Robert F. Kennedy was pronounced dead at 1:44 a.m. on June 6th, nearly 25 hours after the shooting. A worn-out country had to learn how to absorb another terrible loss. We had lost four leaders in just five years, all assassinated, beginning with JFK in '63, then Malcolm X in '65, and finally MLK and RFK in '68.

In some ways, it was hard to stay focused, but once I got to the ballpark, put on my uniform, and watched the fans slowly trickle in, there was an understanding of how important it was that the games went on being played, no matter what. Still, the long fuse of chaos just kept being ignited over and over again.

****

By mid-June, we were a .500 ball club with a 30–30 record, and that summer it seemed to me that baseball was a little bit more important than the previous year. With all the turmoil in the world, baseball was a break from the headlines, if only for a few hours each day. In many ways the slow nature of the game helped tamp down the flames, the unrest in the streets, and the ongoing challenge of civil rights. I have always felt that when fans came to the ballpark and watched greats like Billy Williams, Ernie Banks, Fergie Jenkins, and other players of color, in the same uniform as the white players, working together to win a ball game, it helped level out race relations, because in baseball, the only color that mattered was that of the uniform you were wearing.

My connection to the pitching staff was really growing at that time, and while I still dropped hand signals to call pitches, I had an almost telepathic relationship with whomever was on the mound. Back then we carried 18 pitchers on the staff, and knowing how to work with each of them, their strengths and weaknesses, required a serious amount of trust between me and any particular pitcher. The one guy I was the most connected to was our ace, Ferguson Arthur Jenkins.

In the 1967 season, Fergie won 20 games, had a 2.80 ERA, racked up 236 strikeouts, and came in second for the Cy Young Award. (Mike McCormick of the Giants won.) Additionally, Fergie went to the first of his three All-Star team games. His fastball clocked in consistently around 94 mph and he had a hard slider that was near impossible to hit. Fergie was a power pitcher with incredible command of everything he threw my way. He was so accurate I could have caught him with a pair of pliers, instead of my catcher's mitt.

But that doesn't mean we always agreed on what pitch was needed for a certain hitter.

Many times I would put down a fastball and he'd toss me a curve. There was one time we were playing the Braves at Wrigley and we were up going into the bottom of the 9th inning with me feeling that this game is in the win column. As a matter of fact, I was thinking about getting home for dinner with Betty and the kids. Next thing I know, the bases are loaded, and we were up by one run. I called for a curve ball, and Fergie launched a fastball that sailed over my head to the screen behind home plate, and the tying run scores. I'm not about to go to the mound and talk with him, because he isn't gonna listen to me anyway. I called another curve on the next hitter, Jenkins threw a fastball right down the middle of the plate, the batter smacked a single, and we lost the game. In the post-game show, Jack Brickhouse asked Jenkins who is the toughest player in the league he has to pitch to.

Fergie quickly responds with, *"My catcher, Randy Hundley."*

He was the first pitcher in MLB history to record more than 3,000 strikeouts (3,192) with fewer than 1,000 walks (997) in his career. I have to give credit to Durocher, who saw raw potential in Fergie when he came to the Cubs from the Phillies in 1966.

Leo moved Fergie out of the bullpen as a reliever to a starter, and he never looked back.

That 1968 season was also a great year for Fergie, who pitched in 40 games, won 20 and lost 15, had an impressive 2.63 ERA, and struck out 260 batters. I loved getting a 3–2 count on a batter and calling for that fastball that moved so well in the zone. Even though the hitter knew what was coming, he either missed it or simply watched it rocket past the plate, into my mitt, and to getting called out on strikes, another notch on Fergie's belt. When it was all said and done, Fergie spent 20 years in the majors: 10 years with the Cubs, 6 in Texas, 2 in Philadelphia, and 2 in Boston. He also threw 140 complete games in his career, which would be impossible to do in today's game, as it's become so specialized in terms of pitching. Fergie's best single-game performance came in the 1967 All-Star Game when he struck out six of the top sluggers in the American League: Harmon Killebrew, Tony Conigliaro, Mickey Mantle, Jim Fregosi, Rod Carew, and Tony Oliva, in that order. Fergie won the Cy Young in 1971 and as a hitter, Jenkins posted a lifetime .165 batting average (148-for-896) with 54 runs, 13 home runs, 85 RBI, and 41 bases on balls. Defensively, he recorded a .954 fielding percentage. Impressive stats for a pitcher and because of all that and more, Ferguson Arthur Jenkins was inducted into Cooperstown as part of the Class of 1991 and was the first Canadian in the Hall of Fame. I am so honored to have been on the receiving end of 188 of his total games pitched, more than any other catcher in his long and historic career. It was the Chicago Cubs' only other Gold Glove–winning backstop, Jody Davis, who caught Fergie's 3,000[th] strikeout.

The Cubs eventually retired his #31 jersey in 2009, and while most of us were working offseason jobs, Fergie was playing basketball with the Harlem Globetrotters from 1967 to 1969. Not too bad for a guy who perfected his pitching skills by throwing lumps of coal at passing railroad cars in Chatham, Ontario, as a kid.

Ron Santo, Don Kessinger, and Billy Williams were all named to the 1968 All-Star team that year, with Santo and Kessinger in the starting lineup. It was the first game to be played at night, under the lights in the Astrodome, the place where Leo loved to launch dugout phones. The National League defeated the American League 1–0 as Willie Mays scored the only run needed in the 1st inning, after pitcher Luis Tiant attempted a pickoff that went bad and it got away from Harmon Killebrew at first base. Willie took second and was brought home by Willie McCovey, the batter that most teams created "The Shift," for to right field, as he was a dead pull-hitter. I remember watching the game on television back home and being so proud of the guys being named to the All-Star team, after scraping the bottom of the barrel for so long as a ballclub.

After the break, it was back to the business of baseball, and the second half of the season really started taking a toll on my body, as the hotter months of the season drained me. In 1968, I caught 160 games (147 were complete games) and set a new league record. No MLB player has caught more than 150 games in a season since Brad Ausmus in 2000, and the 150-game mark has only been broken 27 times in major league history. The 160 games I caught in 1968 stand as the most in league history for defensive games at catcher. Putting that gear on day in and day out, taking the foul tips and constant crouching, even barking at umps, all sapped my energy. Except for a few players, it's no wonder that most catchers are not known for their batting average because the position demands so much of you. By the time you are in the batter's box, you've been in on more plays than anyone else on the field, except for the pitcher.

****

We were on a West Coast road trip in late August, playing against the Astros, Giants, and Dodgers, when we heard about the riots in Chicago during the 1968 Democratic National Convention. The news reports were showing scenes of total mayhem from August 23rd to the 28th as police clashed with anti-war protesters. The news cameras were rolling live around the nation, as thousands of people flooded the streets, showing scenes of police violence against protesters, reporters, photographers, and bystanders that were later described by the National Commission on the Causes and Prevention of Violence as a "police riot." Mayor Richard J. Daley was quoted as saying, *"The police aren't there to create disorder, they are there to preserve disorder."* That statement pretty much summed up the feeling in Chicago at the time: chaos and disorder in the streets. This great city had become a war zone of its own, as if we needed another one.

But at "The Friendly Confines," fans could take a break, sit back and soak up the sun, and have their pencil and scorecards ready as we continued our race for the pennant. Despite 32 home runs from Banks, 30 from Williams, and 26 from Santo, a much-improved defense, along with great production from our pitchers Jenkins, Hands, Nye, Niekro, and Holtzman, we finished in third place for a second year in a row. The Cubs ended up with an 84–78 record, 9 games back from the second-place Giants, and a full 13 games behind the St. Louis Cardinals, who lost the World Series in 7 games to the Detroit Tigers.

Even though we came in third, momentum was building, our confidence was growing, and we felt that our time was close and that maybe 1969 would be the year.

The best of the best—Fergie Jenkins—1968

-5-
CUB POWER!

Opening Day, April 8, 1969, is etched in my mind. It's the game that started the most memorable season of my career and lit the fuse of an unforgettable, explosive season of baseball, both on and off the field.

The ballpark was packed with 40,796 Cubs fans, made up of a mixture of school kids who ditched class, those long-suffering fans who always made it to the first game no matter how bad the previous season ended, and adults who played hooky from work, so they could feel like kids again, if only for a few hours.

We had Fergie on the mound who was coming off two great seasons, and as a team, we were rested up and healthy. We were playing the Philadelphia Phillies, who had Chris Short on the hill. In the top of the 1st inning, the Phillies scored a run when Larry Hisle found his way home after reaching first base on a bunt single and got moved around until he crossed the plate.

To lead off the Cubs half of the 1st inning, Kessinger struck out, Beckert and Williams both followed with singles, Santo hit a ground ball, moving Beck to third, but Williams was a force out at second. Ernie Banks came up and proceeded to hit a line shot deep into the left field bleachers, his first round-tripper of the year, and we were then up 3–1 and Wrigley Field erupted with cheers.

Eventually, the Phillies added some runs, including a three-run dinger from Don Money, and we were tied in the 9th inning 5–5. The Phillies broke the tie in the 11th, and were up 6–5 as we came up for our last wraps in the bottom half of the inning.

Ernie led off with a deep fly to left that was caught on the warning track by Johnny Callison for the first out. I dug into the batter's box and worked up a 2–2 count on reliever Barry Lersch and then proceeded to drive a solid single into the gap between center and left field. As I rounded first base, the fans were on their feet yelling, stomping, screaming, like it was a playoff game. First base coach, and my former teammate, Joey Amalfitano, was behind me, hand on my back, saying, *"Reb, get ready to run ..."*

Durocher pulled Jim Hickman and put Willie Smith in to pinch-hit. With one out, and on a 1–0 pitch, Smith proceeded to hammer a fastball into the seats in right center field. The place went wild! On television sets all over Chicago, announcer Jack Brickhouse was screaming, "THAT'S IT! HOME RUN WILLIE SMITH! HEY! HEY! CUBS WIN!" As I ran toward home, the entire team was there to greet me, and when Willie touched the plate, it was pandemonium!

We swept the Phillies in our first homestand to start the season.

It's one of the great moments in my career and would in some ways set the tone for much of the 1969 season. We'd go on to win 11 out of our first 12 games, and once again, Ernie Banks was in front of the cameras with that big grin of his saying, "THE CUBS WILL SHINE IN '69!"

Recalling that season, 54 years later, is bittersweet, to say the least.

My memories of that year are filled with both glorious moments and deeply frustrating ones. A career year in many ways for a team filled with so much talent, determination, and larger-than-life baseball legends, but it would come to be known as the "Most celebrated second-place team in the history of baseball."

****

In 1969, the "Bleacher Bums" became a recognized force in left field. At one game back in 1966, there were fewer than 500 fans in the park, and of those 500, only 23 were in the bleachers, with 14 of them in left field. Of those 14 fans, 10 of them formed the original Bleacher Bums and wore yellow hard hats to identify themselves. The group was started by a bunch of fans led by Mike Murphy (who would go on to become a sports talk host on radio in Chicago) and were originally referred to as "bums" because they seemed to take up residence in the outfield on a consistent basis during the day, and since there were no night games, the conclusion was that they must not have jobs. By '69 their numbers had swelled, and a large platoon of these yellow hard hat–wearing fans had two objectives in life: take whatever steps were needed to help the Cubs win, and to make the opposing team as miserable as possible while they were in town. This was a fun-loving bunch of fans who were led by pitcher Dick Selma, who would whip them into a frenzy from the bullpen by waving a towel over his head when we needed a little extra help on the field. It was a crazy scene at every home game, as the Bleacher Bums packed the outfield and became a serious part of our winning streaks. Rich Nye said that the first time he can ever remember a home run from an opposing team being thrown back on the field was at Wrigley in '69. Hank Aaron launched one deep into the bleachers, and suddenly the ball came flying back on the field, in a straight line toward second base! Soon after, every homer hit by the visiting team started a chant of *"Throw it back! Throw it back!"* and sure enough, the ball would be ejected from the crowd. It's a tradition that continues to this day.

I will also never forget the first time I saw one of the Bleacher Bums in left field waving a Confederate battle flag when I came up to bat. This was a large "Stars and Bars" flag, clearly visible from home plate, 368 feet from the bleachers. Today, that flag is polarizing, to say the least, and is a symbol of hate in many circles. Back then, it was just a fan's way of showing appreciation for my Southern heritage, a symbol of sorts like the yellow hard hats they wore. I never encouraged it nor discouraged it, and in many ways, I am very proud of where and how I grew up, with family values, my faith, and my insistence that all should be treated equally. Many times in my baseball career, I was witness to the Black players being treated as less than I knew they were, and I counted many of them as close friends of mine, brothers in fact, and still do.

In those days, the connection between the ballplayers and fans was much closer than it is today. Without the massive salaries that players get now, many of us worked offseason jobs, which put us in the same working class as many of our fans. One day they would see me behind the plate, knocking down balls in the dirt or tagging out a runner at home, and then a few months later they might run into me at the bank or insurance company I was working for during the offseason. So, it wasn't a surprise when we'd park our cars across the street from Wrigley and be surrounded by fans wishing us well, or have one of the Bleacher Bums put a yellow hard hat on my head and take a picture with me. While the times were full of unrest and tension, the ballpark and all that went with it was a place to leave all the stress behind.

As we racked up the wins, "Cubs Fever" started to spread like wildfire. The legendary broadcaster Jack Brickhouse would say, "The only cure is a pennant!" As it turned out, for most of that season we felt destined to take our place in baseball history, by grabbing the pennant and then going to the World Series. We wanted to be the first Cubs team to do so since the 1945 club, who lost to the Detroit Tigers 4 games to 3 under manager Charlie Grimm.

Among Cubs fans, the 1945 World Series gave birth to what is infamously known as the "Curse of the Goat." As the legend is told, in the fourth game of the World Series, a Chicago tavern owner named Billy Sianis was forced to leave Wrigley Field after showing up with his goat, named "Murphy." After getting kicked out of the park, Sianis's family claims that he sent a telegram to team owner P.K Wrigley which read, *"You are going to lose this World Series and you are never going to win another World Series again. You are never going to win a World Series again because you insulted my goat."* Over the years that goat thing had become a legend in Chicago, and we all knew about it, but as it turned out, a black cat, not a goat, would make its presence known later in the season.

The 1969 season also marked the first year of divisional play in Major League Baseball. The Atlanta Braves and the Cincinnati Reds were placed in the new NL West division, despite being located geographically further east than the Cubs and Cardinals. This was because the New York Mets wanted to be in the same division as the perennial powerhouse Cardinals, in order to compensate for playing fewer games against the Dodgers and Giants during the season. In response, the Cubs demanded to be in the NL East in order to continue playing in the same division as our biggest rivals just down the road in St. Louis. An unintended offshoot of this new alignment was that it set us on a collision course with the Mets. No one could foresee that the Cubs and Mets would play in what is considered one of the greatest pennant races and comebacks in the history of the game.

Looking back at the record books, our 1969 team rivaled any of the great clubs in the game up to that point. We were hitting on all cylinders, so to speak. On June 29th, Billy Williams played his 896th consecutive game against the Cardinals, breaking the NL record held by Stan "the Man" Musial and was on a .293 pace. Beck and Santo were .291, and Don Kessinger would come in at .273 that season. Santo belted 29 home runs, Williams and Hickman both hit 21 round-trippers, and I managed to take 18 balls out of the yard and had a .255 batting average for the year. Even 38-year-old Ernie Banks got in on the action and walloped 23 homers and had 106 RBI.

One of the highlights of that year was on May 28th. I had a huge game at Candlestick Park, the day after my son, Todd, was born. I had three hits in five at-bats, including a double and a grand slam. It was a five RBI day for me, which helped us beat the San Francisco Giants 9–8. Fast forward 27 years later, to 1996 when Todd hit 41 home runs, setting the Mets single-season home-run record (previously set by Darryl Strawberry in 1988) and breaking the single-season record for catchers (previously set by Roy Campanella in 1953). Unfortunately, Betty and I didn't see Todd's record-breaking home run. We were at home and our satellite dish didn't pick up the game. It wasn't until my mom called from Virginia and told us that we found out. During the ceremony at Shea to recognize Todd's achievement, Roy Campanella's widow, Roxie, gave him a picture of the great catcher; it was the last one he ever autographed. Standing on the field, with Todd, Betty, and Roxie, in nearly the same spot where a play at the plate changed our '69 season, was surreal, to say the least.

That year was also my finest in some respects, as I was named to the 1969 All-Star team. Instead of watching the game from home, there I was on the field at RFK Stadium in Washington, DC, along with Santo, Kessinger, Beckert, and Ernie Banks, in front of 45,000 fans in the stadium and millions at home watching on television. The NL beat the AL 9–3 on home runs from Johnny Bench and three dingers from big Willie McCovey, who was also voted the game MVP.

The game was a real kick for me, and a bit surreal when I found myself on the mound in conversation with pitcher Jerry Koosman of the Mets and "Red" Schoendienst, the manager of the Cardinals, who was the NL team manager. Both of them represented our biggest rivalries at that point in the season. It was sure a long way from my early days in the game, and I couldn't help but think about how far I'd come from Bassett High School or wearing Tim Murchison's big pants. Durocher was a bench coach that year, and because the game was played in the middle of the season, it gave him a chance to look for tipoffs from opposing players that we could use for the second half. At that

1969 All-Star Game

point, the Cubs were leading the division with an impressive 63–37–1 record. (On June 6th the game against the Reds ended in a 5–5 tie because of a rainout in the 9th inning.)

****

As the momentum continued into the late summer, "Cubs Fever" kept getting hotter and hotter. Ron Santo started running to the clubhouse after a win and, in the process, would jump and click his heels together, a purely spontaneous move borne out of the joy of victory after losing for so long. A lot of the clubs we beat didn't like it, but Ronnie never meant it as a dig, he was just happy to be winning. Gene Oliver got the idea to capitalize on the "Cubs Fever" thing, and after hearing some of the guys singing in the clubhouse, shower, and on the bus, Ollie found a guy named Peter Wright to produce a record called *Cub Power*. They went to Wrigley and recorded background game sounds from the Bleacher Bums, hot dog vendors, the roaring crowd, and then put together some songs, the greatest of which was "Hey, Hey, Holy Mackerel." As it turned out, Nate Oliver and Willie Smith could really sing, and Santo, Williams, Jenkins, Holtzman, Regan, Hickman, Banks, Kessinger, Popovich, Abernathy, Hands, Qualls, along with announcers Jack Brickhouse and "The Good Kid" Lou Boudreau, either sung backup or took our turn as lead on the vinyl. Across the street from Wrigley at Ray's Bleachers tavern, *Cub Power* was on constant jukebox rotation. When it first came out, you could buy the record for $4.95, and these days they go for well over $100, if you can find one.

The Chicago Cubs Sing

Nate Oliver   Willie Smith   Billy Williams   Ron Santo   Don Kessinger   Randy Hundley   Gene Oliver

Cubs players were everywhere that season, from autograph signings to grand openings of supermarkets and at auto dealerships. A major factor in our popularity was that WGN TV carried the home games back then. Most games had a 1:20 p.m. start (unless it was a doubleheader), and since our lead-in was "Bozo the Clown," we had a huge hold over the audience of younger children. The "Ladies Day" promotion that began in the 1920s by owner William Wrigley Jr. and team president Bill Veeck Sr. took on a whole new dimension. Television sets all over Chicagoland were broadcasting the games to a large female audience who had the game on at home. Add to that when kids were out of school for the summer, we were prime-time viewing. The voices of Jack Brickhouse, Lou Boudreau, Vince Llyod, Lloyd Pettit, and PA announcer Pat Pieper provided the soundtrack for that '69 season. Also, one of my favorite things was taking a side street from Wrigley Field toward the express-way, having legions of young fans waiting at nearly every corner, on my way home, waiting for an autograph. Santo, Beckert, and a few other guys had the same experience.

The weather was heating up, and we were too. Those days, in the middle of summer back in 1969, are some of my best memories, as I got to share them with Betty and my family. She had stood by me for so many ups and downs, losing seasons, moves, and more, and now it was all paying off.

Even though we were having a record season, there was a game in July that was perhaps, an early harbinger of things to come.

****

Don Young, a rich prospect who was becoming a solid ball player at the major league level, started 61 of our first 80 games in center field. We had just lost three out of four to the Cardinals in St. Louis, and our NL East lead shrunk from 8 games to 5½, when we traveled to Shea Stadium to open a series against the Mets on July 8, 1969. Over 55,000 fans crammed into Shea Stadium to watch us go pitch for pitch with the Mets. Fergie was on the mound and had a great game going into the 8th inning, giving up just four hits and one run to the Mets. Ernie and Hickman had both homered off Jerry Koosman, and Beckert drove Jenkins home, after he had drawn a walk-in the top of the 7th. We went into the bottom of the 9th inning up 3–1 and were about to put a much-needed win on the board until Fergie gave up a leadoff hit to Kenny Boswell, a fairly routine fly ball that became a double as the result of Don Young misplaying the ball. One out later, Donn Clendenon stepped in and crushed one on a rope to left center field. It looked like Young snagged the ball, but then he dropped it before crashing into the outfield wall. With Boswell at third base and Clendenon at second, Cleon Jones came up and drove one just out of reach of Billy Williams, scoring both Boswell and Clendenon, and then we were tied 3–3. Wayne Garrett got a single, moving Jones to second base, and then big Ed Kranepool drove home the winning run, and it was game over…or so I thought.

After the game, Durocher publicly blamed Don Young for the loss. Among other comments, Durocher barked, "My (expletive deleted) three-year-old could have caught those balls." While it was a fairly predictable response from Leo, it was actually Ron Santo's comments that caused a stir: "He was just thinking about himself. He had a bad day at the plate, so he's got his head down. He's worrying about his batting average, not the team." After the game, Don dressed and left the clubhouse quickly, and Ron added, "He can keep going out of sight for all I care." The news media captured every word.

That was a very unpredictable response from our team captain.

Ronnie of course realized he had spoken out of anger, apologized to Don personally back at the hotel, and held a press conference the next day to publicly apologize to his teammate. But that was basically the end of Don Young's tenure in center field, as he was immediately replaced by Jimmy Qualls.

Don Young was a fine ballplayer, and a couple of bad plays do not define a career. If that were the case, every time I called for a pitch that got knocked out of the park, I'd be unable to show up for the very next batter. It's a game of breaks, and sometimes they go your way, sometimes they don't. In a twist of fate, the very next night at Shea Stadium ,Tom Seaver was throwing a perfect game going into the bottom of 9th inning, and it was Qualls who broke it up with a bloop single. Seaver ended up with a one-hitter, and the Mets won 4–0.

Such goes the game of baseball.

****

On August 19th Kenny Holtzman threw a no-hitter against the Atlanta Braves. I wasn't behind the plate that day, but instead watching the game from home, recovering from a severed tendon in my toe. Bill Heath filled in and caught seven innings, and then Gene Oliver came in for the last two, as Kenny won the game 3–0. It was a long haul for Holtzman, as he didn't strike out a single Braves player, and that's a lot of trust in your defense. It might have been a different story, had the wind not pushed down a massive shot by Henry Aaron to left field allowing Billy Williams to catch the ball with his back in the ivy.

After Kenny's no-hitter, we had the division lead, up 8½ games over the Cardinals and 9½ over the Mets. By late summer, the Cubs organization was pulling out all stops when it came to rattling our opponents. In late August we were heading to Atlanta to play the Braves ,and unbeknownst to us, Cubs president P.K. Wrigley had invited a bunch of the Bleacher Bums on an all-expenses-paid trip to the series at Atlanta Fulton County

Stadium, just to rile up the Braves. Imported Bleacher Bum Ron Grousl (the same guy who threw back Aaron's homer earlier in the year) dressed up in a bear outfit and did some sort of routine with Braves mascot Chief Noc-A-Homa on the field before the game. He ended up tackling their mascot, then bugged out back to the stands, as the Atlanta crowd sat stunned. Additionally, a few of the Bums were arrested for trying to burn down the Chief's teepee, and one guy was so drunk he fell about 30 feet from the stands to the playing field, but escaped serious injury.

I should have known right then and there it was gonna be a different game in Atlanta.

We were scoreless in the bottom of the 4th inning when Orlando Cepeda hit a double off Kenny Holtzman, which brought tough-hitting Clete Boyer to the plate, who at the time was in a 1–17 slump and needed a hit. But what happened instead is still frozen in my memory.

There was a commotion in the stands, and suddenly this woman started running toward home. I'm in my full squat, getting ready to give Kenny the sign, and all I could see was her bouncing toward the plate as the crowd began to cheer. Next thing I knew, she had her arms around Boyer's neck and was kissing him on the cheek, saying, "Oh Clete! You're the greatest!"

The game had just gone to a whole new level of crazy. Both myself and home-plate ump Paul Pryor just stood there with our mouths hanging open.

"Morgana the Kissing Bandit" had struck again in front of 33,000 fans! Morgana was an exotic dancer in the area, and apparently a week after the smooch heard around the world, Boyer went to the club she danced at, went up on stage when she was doing her routine, kissed her, and said, "Now we're even!"

****

On the other side of the coin, 1969 still had a lot of fires burning, as Vietnam was making headlines every day. National unrest was becoming more apparent and civil rights marches continued as the year went on. Woodstock drew 400,000 people to a dairy farm in upstate New York, Richard Nixon was voted in as president for a second term, and of course the greatest achievement in human history, the Apollo 11 moon landing on July 20th, put everything in perspective.

We were playing the Phillies at Connie Mack Stadium in a doubleheader on that historic day, and as both teams lined up to pay tribute to the astronauts, I kept looking up to the sky thinking to myself that it was hard to believe that a human being was going to set foot on the lunar surface. We took both games from Philadelphia, and just like that rocket that shot men into space, we were surely on our way to the stars or, at least, the postseason and the World Series. After decades of losing and climbing our way out of the baseball standings basement for the past few seasons, this was most assuredly our year.

We would remain in first place for 155 days, setting attendance records at Wrigley, and we were the talk of major league baseball, with all signs pointing to a pennant.

On August 26th, the National League office gave the Chicago Cubs permission to start printing playoff tickets.

And then came September.

-6-
The Tag

On September 8th we limped into Shea Stadium, a bit battered and bruised, having dropped 8 of our previous 13 games, the worst of which was a loss to the Pirates at Wrigley, the day before we played the Mets. We'd just come off a road trip that was plain awful, losing 7 out of 9 games to the Dodgers, Giants, Braves, and Reds. Back at home, with the fantastic Cubs fans to lift us up, we went into that game against the Pirates with a renewed sense of purpose. Even with the road losses, we were still leading the pennant race at that point.

When we got hammered in the first game of the series 13–4, that old familiar feeling crept in, as if we were heading down-hill, with little to stop us. In the second game, "Gentleman" Jim Hickman cranked a homer in the 8th to give us the lead, until Willie Stargell (who of all the men I called pitches against in the majors, might have been the most difficult hitter to retire) parked one in the seats in the top of the 9th, and broke the game open, handing the 7–5 loss to young reliever Ken Johnson.

On the other hand, the Mets had been on a winning streak of sorts, going 9–5 in the same time span. Incredibly, on August 16th we had a 9-game lead in the new NL East division, but even with the slide, we had only lost 3 games in our divisional lead, which made this 2-game series with NY, all-important, and we went into Shea with a 2½ game lead over the Mets.

Even if the Mets swept us, we would still have a slight lead, but of course, we couldn't fathom a sweep, even though we weren't playing our best ball.

The long season had begun to take a toll on all of us, as Leo rarely platooned his star players. I guess he figured that he wasn't going to mess around with the lineup that had won 11 out of its first 12 games and had been leading the NL East for 155 days, until we hit a brick wall in September. I had dropped weight, my arm ached, and my knees were starting to feel like rusted hinges after squatting behind the plate without a break. The rest of the guys were running on fumes as well.

****

It was a pitchers' duel from the get-go. We had my partner from the 1966 Giants trade, Bill Hands, on the mound, and the Mets put up Jerry Koosman, a fine southpaw who was on his way to an All-Star season, boasting a 2.28 ERA and would eventually log in 180 strikeouts in 1969. On our side, Hands was no slouch: in the '69 season he was a 20-game winner, with a 2.49 ERA, 18 complete games, and a total of 300 innings pitched that year.

Basically, it was two of the game's best going at it head-to-head, pitch-for-pitch, and we knew it would be a heavyweight contender fight. We had everything to lose; the Mets had everything to gain.

In the 1st inning, Koosman struck out Kessinger, Beckert, and Williams to start the game. I figured we needed to send a message to the Mets, that while we might have been down, we weren't out, so I had Bill Hands bring one high and tight to the Mets leadoff hitter, Tommie Agee.

Hand's fastball put Agee flat on his fanny, right in the box, after some serious chin music. It was important to establish the fact that we were still the division leaders, and needed to play like it. I had no way of knowing what a great game Agee would have, and perhaps that first pitch lit a fuse of sorts, as he would figure prominently in one of the most controversial calls in the history of baseball just a few innings later.

In the 2nd inning, Koosman retaliated with a pitch that hammered Santo in the wrist, which sent Ronnie to first base in serious pain. I thought he might have broken bones in his hand, but he stayed in and played through it. When I asked him about it later, he said that he didn't think it was intentional, and if he had, he might have done something about it. With Santo on first, Koosman proceeded to strike out Banks, Hickman, and myself to end the inning.

Bud Harrelson started off the bottom of the 3rd with an infield single. Koosman hit a pop-up foul ball out to Ernie, which brought Agee to the plate. Tommie proceeded to hit a fastball off Hands that landed deep into the seats at Shea, giving them a 2–0 lead. We came back in the 6th to tie it up, off singles by Kessinger and Beckert, followed by a single from Billy Williams that brought Kessinger home and a sac fly from Santo that got Beckert home, and we tied the game 2–2.

It was in the bottom of the 6th inning when arguably the most controversial call at the plate in the history of baseball took place.

No way around it, Agee was having one heck of a game. After his homer in the 3rd, he followed it with a double off Hands in the Mets half of the 6th. I clearly remember thinking that Tommie was "in the zone," and no matter what pitch I called for, he was going to figure out a way to hit it. With Agee standing on second, rookie Wayne Garrett walked to the plate, and quite frankly, I wasn't too worried. Garrett, a light-hitting left-hander, had launched two shallow fly balls to right field, causing no damage in his previous plate appearances. As he came to the box, the lights of Shea Stadium began to illuminate the field, something we never had to deal with at Wrigley, as there wouldn't be night baseball at "The Friendly Confines" until 1988.

Garrett proceeded to punch a single to the right side, smack-dab between Beckert and Banks. Neither of them was able to knock it down, and I knew there was no way that Agee was going to stop at third for any reason. Jim Hickman scooped the ball on two hops in short right field and fired a laser strike toward home plate as Agee was coming down the third base line like a bullet. I tossed off my mask and steadied myself for what I thought for sure was to be a collision at the plate. Behind me, in the Mets on-deck circle, I could hear Donn Clendenon yelling at Agee to hit the dirt and slide into home, as he could clearly see the throw from Hick was going to beat Tommie to the plate.

I heard the *thump* of the ball in my mitt while Agee was five strides away from home, and I turned toward him, in perfect alignment for a tag. My left leg was blocking the plate (allowable then) and I tagged Tommie so hard, I almost lost the ball, but it stuck in the top of the webbing of the glove, and I immediately turned back toward the field, keeping an eye on Garrett. It was a bang-bang play, and I had zero doubt that Agee was out.

That's when I knew something was wrong.

In the stands, 43,274 crazed New York Mets fans were on their feet screaming, as rookie umpire Satch Davidson had called Agee safe!

My instincts took over, and I forgot all about the rookie at first, and turned my attention to the rookie ump! I was furious! How could he have missed that call? But mad as I was, I knew that if I touched him in any way (and boy did I want to), I would be thrown out of the game. I knew I had tagged him cleanly, but somehow Davidson didn't see it. If we had Instant Replay back then, Agee would be called out right then and there, no doubt.

But we didn't.

In a flash, Leo was standing next to me as I started barking at Davidson, making sure I didn't bump the ump and get tossed from the game. When I finished ranting and raving, Davidson said, "Is that all you got, Randy?" I screamed, "No, man, I ought to bite your head off!" Davidson responded with, *"Well if you did that, Randy, you'd have more brains in your stomach than you have in your head."*

As the Mets fans continued to roar, I instantly knew deep down, that on some level, that play was the defining moment of the 1969 season.

We had been riding high for so long, even though going into New York with the Mets right on our heels, we still felt somewhat invincible, and perhaps in some ways ordained, that this was *our year*.

That missed call by Davidson has been replaying in my mind, over and over and over again, for the past 50-plus years. I still think about how things might have been different had Agee been called out. I've thought about it, talked about it, been interviewed about it, and now I'm writing about it, and it *still burns my hillbilly fanny*.

Perhaps the momentum would not have swung toward the Mets, and we would have remained tied 2–2 and perhaps that call in our favor just might have turned the tide back our way. But baseball is a game of "what ifs" that can be pondered, argued, and dissected long after the game is over.

In some ways, that blown call was a harbinger of things to come, as Mets hurler Jerry Koosman got the win, Bill Hands took the loss, and we dropped the game 3–2. To make matters worse, the next day we faced Tom Seaver, over 50,000 Mets fans—and the infamous black cat.

"The Black Cat" incident seemed to put the final stamp on our season.

First off, Leo had to put Fergie on the mound with just two days' rest, and even though he was our best pitcher, that's asking a lot, for a guy who would routinely go the distance. The deal was that Kenny Holtzman had to miss the game for the Jewish New Year, Rosh Hashanah, so he was out of the lineup, but the Mets had the rested and fresh Tom Seaver on the mound.

Playing under the lights, we were just into the top of the 4th inning and Billy Williams was at the plate when a stray black cat suddenly appeared on the field, for all the world to see. While the Met fans roared, the cat started circling Santo, who was waiting in the on-deck circle, and Santo barked out, "Oh man ... we're screwed now," and the cat proceeded to prance around a bit in front of our dugout, which sent Durocher into fits. Leo kept yelling for someone to get the cat away from him, as if it knew how superstitious he was. I can't imagine what that black cat did to his mind. I was sitting on the bench thinking to myself, "This can't be happening," but it was.

After surveying the scene, the cat quickly disappeared, but on some level, that old wives' tale of a black cat crossing your path (or in our case, the dugout) being bad luck ran through my mind. Some people suspected that a NY fan dumped the cat on the field, but Mets slugger Ed Kranepool said he saw cats all the time at Shea because the place had a substantial rat population, which doesn't surprise me.

Adding insult to injury, in the 7th inning the lights went out at Shea Stadium, and the massive crowd started to wave white towels and in unison began singing, *"Bye-bye Leo, bye-bye Leo, we hate to see you go."* With Durocher fuming, we all sat there on the bench watching our playoff hopes slowly swirl down the drain. We lost that second game 7–1 to the Mets, and the implosion of the last month of the 1969 season would be unrecoverable for the Cubs.

In many ways, "The Tag" was a pivotal moment, a representation of the slow erosion of our season, played out in New York against our biggest rivals—the Mets.

We left New York with a ½ game lead and headed to Philadelphia to face the Phillies, who were having a terrible season. But they rose to the occasion and we dropped both games to them, and I recall an especially painful moment in the second game when Dick Selma threw a surprise pick-off attempt to Santo at third, but unfortunately, Selma never let Ronnie in on the play. The ball scooted down the left field line, opening up a rally for the Phillies. In contrast, there were fewer than 5,000 in attendance at old Connie Mack Stadium, but it still felt like 50,000.

****

In all fairness, the Mets had one heck of a ballclub, and I gotta give credit where it's due. Their pitching staff was stellar, with Jerry Koosman, Don Cardwell, Tug McGraw, a young Nolan Ryan, and their ace Tom Seaver. Big bats from Ron Swaboda, Donn Clendenon, Kenny Boswell, Ed Kranepool, and of course Tommie Agee. Behind the plate, Jerry Grote was a fixture, and while Leo had been running at full speed with our starters, the Mets had been platooning guys in and out all season. After the Mets won the World Series, I caught a stat from a NY sports reporter that recorded the difference between the number of games our starters played vs. the number of games the Mets players were in. In seven of the eight starting positions, we played *16 games more per man* than the Mets did in rotation. By the time August rolled around, we were sagging, by September we were dragging, and it showed up both on and off the field.

The Mets were getting their second wind and starting to smell the finish line, as we were starting to gasp for air. Revisionist history suggests that if Mets skipper Gil Hodges was managing the Cubs that year, it would have had a better outcome for us, as he had a reputation for being a calming influence in the clubhouse, whereas Durocher was just the opposite. Also, the fact that Hodges rested his guys more often, which made a big difference, is hard to argue.

Even though we would end up with a 92–70 record, we lost 17½ games to the Mets in the standings during the last quarter of the season. You can't drop that many games and come out on top.

That team from New York would go on to become "The Miracle Mets" with a record of 100–62 and would defeat the Atlanta Braves in three games in the National League Championship Series and become the World Series champs after battling the Baltimore Orioles. They were the first expansion team to hit the "trifecta," which includes a division title, pennant, and World Series, after just eight years as a ballclub, proving that it's not where you start that matters most, but where you finish. As a side note, years later, before he passed away in 2001, Tommie admitted I had tagged him out, but I already knew that.

****

Despite the disappointing end to the 1969 season, I often wonder if our team, with four future Hall of Famers—Ferguson Jenkins, Ernie Banks, Ron Santo, and Billy Williams—along with an incredible supporting cast of players like Kessinger, Beckert, Holtzman, Nye, Popovich, Hickman, Young, Abernathy, Regan, and Selma, would even be as remembered as we have been. Not for winning it all, but coming up short, after such an incredible season.

Of all the difficult things I remember from that season, the guy I felt really bad for was Ernie Banks. He'd accomplished so much in his career, and a World Series would have been a capstone on his great time in baseball. Despite the way the year turned out, Ernie said that 1969 was the favorite out of his 19 seasons in major league baseball, and that is saying a lot about our team, the fans, and the incredible ride we had that summer.

The 1969 Chicago Cubs

-7-
A NEW DECADE

By 1970 the war in Vietnam had reached its peak, and on many levels, the civil rights marches had as well. The turbulent 1960s had come to an end, and people were ready for a new direction after so much unrest. The Cubs were gearing up for a winning season, after the sting of the previous campaign.

We won our final game of 1969 against the Mets, but it was little consolation to the team, the fans, and the City of Chicago. The winter that followed was a long one; I rested up, had some great family time with Betty and the kids, and as spring rolled around, I was really looking forward to the 1970 season.

The core of the team was mostly intact: Jenkins, Hands, Holtzman, and Regan were on the mound and Santo, Kessinger, Beckert, and Banks returned to the infield. Hickman, Williams, and Spangler were in the outfield, but in the offseason, Oscar Gamble and Dick Selma were traded away, and we would lose Jimmy Qualls, Ted Abernathy, Don Young, and Archie Reynolds along the way. We added Milt Pappas and perhaps the most colorful and animated ball player I've ever known, Joe Pepitone, was purchased from the Houston Astros.

****

Pepitone was signed by the New York Yankees as a free agent in 1958. He broke in with the Yankees in 1962, backing up the legendary Moose Skowron at first base. The rumor was that Pepi spent his entire $25,000 signing bonus while on his way to spring training. It wouldn't surprise me if this story was true. He also won a World Series ring with the Yankees in his rookie year. Not a bad start.

He came to the Cubs in July of the 1970 season and took over for Hickman in center field, moving Jimmy to first base and effectively putting Banks on the bench. Change is always difficult in baseball, especially when you are talking about a living legend at the time, which Banks was. But Ernie was on the downside of his career and would retire in 1971.

With his long sideburns and swagger, Pepitone rubbed Durocher the wrong way from day one. The tactics Leo used to push us in previous years had zero effect on Pepi, who wasn't having any of it. One day I got a message to meet Leo in his office and my heart sank. I was thinking to myself that he was trading me, but when I got there, I found out pretty quickly that he had something else on his mind. "Come here, let me show you something," Leo barked. We stepped outside of his office, and there, not ten feet away, was Pepitone's motorcycle. "You see this thing? This machine? This is why he's not hitting as well as he could. His hands are working those handles and it's messing up his wrists!"

Pepitone had Leo's number from that point on.

He kept parking that motorcycle right outside of Durocher's door, and he'd give it a little extra on the engine every time he started that thing up. I can just imagine Leo sitting at his desk, teeth clenched in anger when Pepi hit the throttle. Pepitone publicly admitted to drug use in his career, and despite that, he would earn three Gold Glove Awards, and go to three All-Star games. He was truly one of a kind, and I had more fun watching Joe (on and off the field) over the years, more than just about any other player in the game. Every now and then we were roommates on the road, and Pepi's lifestyle made this country boy blush more than a few times.

Joe Pepitone

****

I was all geared up for a great year in 1970, and then late in spring training, I got hurt. It was a preseason game against the Oakland A's, and I got a chip fracture of my thumb on a play at the plate, which caused me to miss the season-opening road trip to Philadelphia and Montreal (the new expansion team). I was back behind the dish for the home opener against the Phillies on April 14th, but on April 21st I sustained torn cartilage in my left knee after Cardinals player Carl Taylor collided with me at home plate. That knocked me out of the game and for a big chunk of the season, as I would only play in 73 games that year.

My injury prompted the Cubs to trade Randy Bobb for the Mets backup catcher, J.C. Martin. J.C. and I came from the same county back in Virginia, but he attended rival Drury Mason High and was a star basketball player and baseball player for them. Rockford, Illinois, native Ken Rudolph also joined the Cubs, and he provided solid backup behind the plate. On May 12th, the same day that Ernie Banks hit his 500th home run, the Cubs acquired catcher Jack Hiatt from the Expos for a young outfielder named Boots Day. In 1970, Hiatt would play in 66 games for the Cubs, with a record of 43 hits, 2 home runs, and 22 RBI.

I cannot begin to tell you how difficult it was for me to be injured and not playing. As the guy who called pitches from behind the plate for years, I felt disconnected from the game, my teammates, and all that goes along with it. The saving grace was, of course, Betty. She tended to my needs, urged me on, supported me in every way. When I needed it the most, her faith helped me find mine. When the press asked Durocher about losing his catcher, he replied, "You cannot replace Randy Hundley. His absence means at least ten games lost, if not more, in the standings. He's that much of an impact on the field and off. No one ran on him when he was catching, and he was a good hitter. They took away more than just a catcher. They took away my field general out there."

Nevertheless, baseball isn't about one player, and the Cubs had a great spring, and by April 30th we were 13–5, finishing the month 2½ games in first place, and comparisons to the 1969 season started all over again. (The next time a Cubs team had an April record like that wasn't until 2020.) However, that accomplishment was marred a bit, as the fans had picked up where they left off in 1969. As each home game was played, the crowd got more and more out of hand. They were throwing trash on the field, jumping out of the stands, and interrupting the games. Soon the now-famous chain-link basket was installed to keep fans from throwing stuff on the field (even though they kept trying), and the club even mortared concrete blocks and triangles on the top of the walls to prevent people from walking on them.

We continued to play solid ball, and even though we lost Ted Abernathy to Kansas City, we ended May still in first place. But then we lost 12 in a row in June, including 5 games to the Mets, giving the division lead over to New York. Right around that time, controversy hit, as it turned out that Durocher was withholding various bits of information from the media and players, only to reveal his thoughts one night on his evening radio show in Chicago. Leo had made many appearances on radio and television shows like *Mr. Ed* and *The Munsters* and never met a microphone he didn't like. He apparently decided to use his radio show to inform Cubs fans that he was going to bench Santo (who only found out by listening to the show), which didn't go over too well with Ronnie. He also said he planned to platoon Banks and Hickman and called Jim "My hillbilly."

Of course, the Chicago sports reporters and fans had a field day with all of this.

Shortly after, Leo gave up his radio show to focus on managing, which was a good move all the way around, but there was collateral damage that couldn't be fully repaired, just like my knee. No matter how much I worked it, and trained on it, it was never the same, and in some way, shape, or form, Leo's relationship with the team wouldn't be like it was in the previous years.

Later in the '70 season, someone started sending Ron Santo death threats, a situation the Cubs and the FBI took seriously, claiming he would be shot at Shea Stadium during our upcoming series with the Mets. His roommate, Glenn Beckert, didn't take the threat as seriously but, just in case, put up a sign over his hotel bed that said, "Beckert Sleeps Here" with an arrow pointing down and one that read, "Santo Sleeps Here" over Ron's bed, just in case a would-be assassin should need to make a choice. The FBI even had a guy pose as Ron undercover, but no attempts were made. Not long after, Santo came into the clubhouse at Wrigley to get dressed for a game and there was a big sack of mail next to his locker. One by one guys were walking by saying, *"Do you hear something ticking?"* That sent Ron into a frenzy, and he started digging in the bag until he came up with a box with no return address on it that was definitely ticking.

Without opening it, he ran out of the clubhouse and onto the field, then tossed the package halfway to the left field bleachers waiting for an explosion! When the box didn't blow up, Ron came back to the clubhouse with all of us doubled over in laughter. As it turned out, Billy and Beck had swiped the trainer's timer, set the dial so it started to *tick ... tick ... tick ...*, put it in a plain brown paper–wrapped box, and planted it in the bag.

I don't think Ronnie thought it was as funny as we did.

Oddly enough, there were more death threats against Santo in 1972, and then after that it stopped. Ronnie figured whomever was jerking his chain must have kicked off or moved on to someone else.

****

By the time the end of June rolled around, we had given up the division lead to the Mets, were 3½ games out of first, and were in third place. We started July by picking up pitcher Juan Pizzaro, and I was finally able to rejoin the team. For the 1970 All-Star game, Kessinger and Becket, along with Jim Hickman (who was having a great year), were the only players representing the Cubs. Durocher was a bench coach again, and the NL beat the AL 5–4 in front of 50,000 fans at Riverfront Stadium. The winning run scored in the bottom of the 12th inning when Jimmy Hickman hit a single to center, sending Pete Rose toward home, who then proceeded to hammer Cleveland catcher Ray Fosse at the plate and secure the victory. There's an interesting side story to that collision. The night before the game, Rose was scheduled to have dinner with Sam McDowell, a friend and All-Star pitcher for the Cleveland Indians. A couple weeks before the game, McDowell called Rose and asked if he could bring Fosse with him to dinner, as the young catcher had just been named to the All-Star team. Rose agreed and recalls that most of the night the rookie Fosse wanted to know all he could about Johnny Bench (Pete's teammate on the Reds) who had been named Rookie of the Year in '68 and was beginning to establish himself as one of the premiere catchers in the league. Not sure what the odds are that Fosse had any idea that the next night, the guy who bought him dinner, would hit him like a freight train at home plate. Predictably, Ray was injured on the play, but the first X-rays revealed no fractures or other damage. But a reexamination the following year revealed Fosse had sustained a fractured and separated shoulder, which healed incorrectly, causing chronic pain that never entirely resolved itself, severely affecting his career. Such is the life of a major league catcher. Since that time, the rules have changed about those types of plays. The MLB Rulebook states: "The baserunner is not allowed to deviate from his direct path to initiate contact with the catcher (or any player covering the plate). Runners are considered to be in violation of this rule if they collide with the catcher in cases where a slide could have been used to avoid the collision." Back then, it was the most dangerous position in baseball. To his credit, Fosse would go on to win Gold Gloves in 1970 and '71 as the best catcher in the American League.

By August things were tightening up, with a three-team race beginning to take form. The Pirates were in first, Mets in second, and we were sitting in third place, 5½ games out. We had a great road trip to the West Coast, which included a sweep of the Padres, and by the first week of September, we were sitting in second place, just one game behind the Pirates. For the rest of the month, it was a constant back and forth between the Cubs and Mets for second place in the NL East. On September 3rd, Billy Williams asked Leo for a day off. The constant battering of the game caught up with him, and he needed a breather. Billy ended his streak of 1,117 games in a row (a National League record at the time), and to this day, he has the sixth-longest streak of games played in major league history.

Hall of Famer Billy Williams

A pivotal game was on September 13th, when we were playing the first-place Pirates. We had slipped back to third behind the

Mets, just one game out of the lead, and we were losing 2–1 with two outs in the bottom of the 9th inning. Willie Smith came in to pinch-hit for Bill Hands, who had gone the distance. Smith hit a routine fly ball to center field, which should have ended the game, but Matty Alou dropped the ball and Smith had a double on Alou's error. Leo sent Kenny Rudolph in to pinch-run, then Kessinger proceeded to hit a clutch single, scoring Rudolph from second, tying the game 2–2. Beck came up and he got a single that pushed Kessinger to second base. Then Billy Williams stepped to the plate and proceeded to slam a ball in the gap between left and center, off Pirate's pitcher Steve Blass, and Kessinger scored from second. We won in the bottom of the 9th, 3–2. If we would have lost that game, that was season over then and there for us, but like so many times in baseball, you never know how it will turn out, until the last out.

In September, we added batting champ Tommy Davis and pitcher Hoyt Wilhelm in an attempt to prop up our chances of winning a pennant. But when it was all said and done, the '70 Cubs came in second place, five games in back of the Pirates, who lost the NLCS to the "Big Red Machine" Cincinnati Reds, who then lost the World Series to the Baltimore Orioles in five games. "The Miracle Mets" finished in third after their spoiler run in 1969, and one game behind us in the standings, which in some way was small satisfaction after the prior year.

****

While it was a difficult year for me physically, I was still ranked the #1 catcher in the National League by sportswriters, followed by Johnny Bench, Jerry Grote, and Manny Sanguillén. The 1970 season was also the year in which Billy Williams knocked out 42 home runs, Jim Hickman hit 32 home runs, Ron Santo hit 26 home runs, and Johnny Callison had 19 dingers. That same summer Ernie became the 9th player to hit 500 home runs. The pitching was fairly stable behind Fergie's 22 wins, Bill Hands's 18 wins, Holtzman's 17 wins, and Pappas rounding out the season with 10 games in the win column.

I was more than ready to have some time off and rest up. While I was busy with offseason stuff, Betty was scouting out a possible new place for us, and one day she found the perfect home. It was time for something that fit our growing family, and thinking that I wasn't going anywhere and that I would always be playing for the Cubs, it seemed like the right decision.

****

The 1971 season was the 100th year for the Chicago Cubs as a franchise, and once again, I felt rested and ready. But during a routine run-down play at spring training against the California Angels, my right knee went out on me again. I got on the rehab routine, missed the opener that year, but came back on May 12th, only to reinjure that knee again. Two weeks later, I made another attempt to come back by wearing a special knee brace, but had to be carried off the field on a stretcher, after hitting a routine pop fly and my knee just gave out. It was becoming apparent to me that the hundreds of games behind the plate, and the collisions at home, had begun to take a serious toll. On June 3rd I underwent surgery to fix a torn cruciate ligament and ended up having an acute gall bladder attack. I was in bad shape, and a hospital representative told the press, "We almost lost him."

I played a total of nine games in 1971.

The upside was that I carried a .350 batting average, the down-side is that I only stepped to the plate 20 times that year. The other catchers filled in, with a majority of games caught by Chris Cannizzaro, who came over from the Padres. J.C. Martin caught 47 games, and Ken Rudolph handled 25 games. It was the year that Ernie Banks said goodbye to baseball, Billy hit 28 home runs, Ronnie added 21 more, along with Joe Pepitone hitting 16 home runs. Even though we came in third place that year, Beck, Jenkins, Santo, and Don Kessinger made the All-Star team. This time the AL won 6–4, their first win since 1962, and it would be their last until 1982.

Then, on August 23rd, an explosion happened in the clubhouse.

Leo came up to me and said, "Randy, I'm calling a meeting and I want you to go find Pepitone and tell him to sit there and not say anything." I had no idea what was going on, but I took off looking for Pepi. I finally tracked him down by the smell of weed and found him sitting in a bathroom stall, pants around his ankles, smoking a joint. So Joe finished up and followed me back to the meeting. When Leo was done with his ranting and raving, he asked if anyone had anything to say. Milt Pappas got up, because he's the player rep, and he made a few comments, and then Pepitone raised his hand, which in turn raised Leo's blood pressure. "Hey, Leo, Ralph Houk doesn't manage this way . . . *what's your deal*?" You could have heard a pin drop, and I'm thinking, "What the crap, Pepi? Just sit there and keep your mouth shut." There's a lot of barking back and forth, and eventually John Holland, the Cubs GM, is called down to the meeting. Things went from bad to worse when the conversation around the upcoming "Ron Santo Day" ended in a shouting match between Santo and Leo. A couple guys had to restrain Ronnie, who wanted to get his hands on Durocher. Leo left the meeting threatening to quit, Santo felt betrayed, and all the while it was Pepi who lit the fuse, and he just kinda sat back and watched the show.

Worst clubhouse meeting…*ever.*

But in spite of all the behind-the-scenes commotion, on August 28, 1971, over 35,000 fans packed Wrigley Field for "Ron Santo Day," and Ronnie used the platform to go public with the fact he was a diabetic. "I didn't want anyone else to know about this originally. I'm a diabetic and had a full career in the major leagues and a darned good one," Ronnie said in a pregame ceremony hosted by the great Cubs broadcaster Jack Brickhouse. "The reason I've done so well is I've accepted it and learned to live with it. I feel strongly we're going to find a cure for this."

That night Pepitone was so proud to be the toastmaster at a $50 per plate fundraiser held at the Pick-Congress Hotel. Also, the sale of Ron Santo Day buttons raised over $7,000 for diabetes research. Something that started out to be a terrible interaction between Durocher and Santo became a blessing in disguise. Pepi could be a pain in the fanny, but in the end, he really stood up for Ronnie when he needed it most.

By the of the 1971 season, I'd been playing baseball for a dozen years, and while I was still mentally at the big-league level, I became more conscious of my eroding physical skills due to injury. My knees were starting to give out, and while I was able to rehab in the offseason, I was growing more and more concerned about my impending retirement from baseball. I didn't know much further I could go.

****

I bounced back a bit in 1972 and was behind the plate for 114 games that year. Of course, changes to the team were inevitable.

After the 1971 season, Kenny Holtzman was traded to Oakland for outfielder Rick Monday. Holtzman felt he had taken a brunt of Durocher's tirades and asked for a trade, which severely diminished our pitching ranks. The 1972 season was the first time in 19 seasons that Ernie Banks wouldn't be on the field in a Cubs uniform. Even still, I managed to lead all catchers in the National League with a .995 fielding percentage in '72 and hammered a grand slam off Giants' pitcher Don Carrithers on June 20th.

That ball is long gone! Hey! Hey!

But the high point for me was catching two no-hitters in '72, one of only a half-dozen catchers in MLB history to catch two in one season. A no-hitter is rare, and of this writing, there have only been 322 no-hitters officially recognized by Major League Baseball. On April 16th the first no-hitter was thrown by rookie phenom Burt "Happy" Hooton in his fourth start as a pro pitcher, and remarkably, Burt never played a single inning of minor league ball. I can tell you that Burt's knuckle-curve was right up there with the guy I had to face in my second at-bat, Sandy Koufax and his curve ball. Hooton's pitch was near impossible to hit, and not that much fun to catch. I had a busy day behind the plate because Burt's ball started out at your head and dropped like a stone to the dirt. The upside of the win was that P.K. Wrigley gave Burt a $2,500 raise, and I got a $500 bonus because it was the first time I caught a no-hitter.

The second no-no was with Milt Pappas, on September 2nd in an 8–0 route over the Padres. That game was controversial, to say the least. Milt had a perfect game going, as he retired 26 Padres in a row and then in the 9th inning, Larry Stahl drew a walk, which of course ticked off Pappas, who thought he should have had at least one of those balls called a strike. Matter of fact, on the second pitch Milt came off the mound a couple of steps toward home, which never is a good idea. Bruce Froemming was behind the plate as a second-year ump and said, "Randy, if he takes one more step, he's gone from the game." So, I went out and settled Milt down and said, "Brother, let it go, you've got a no-no going here, don't let a couple of pitches change that." We worked to a full count and then Froemming called ball four. Milt came off the mound again, barking at the ump, and I had to set his fanny back on the pitching rubber. Pappas took a couple of deep breaths and then the next batter, Gerry Jestadt, popped a ball into short right field. Carmen Fanzone caught it, preserving Milt's no-hitter, which was the 197th win of his career. In the end, Milt won 209 games, was a two-time All-Star, and had 43 shut-outs in his 17-year career, which is an incredible legacy.

Post-game smiles after Milt's no-hitter

On Saturday July 26th, we played the Dodgers at Wrigley and beat them 3–2 in 11 innings, when I drove in the winning run with a bases-loaded single. However, Leo Durocher wasn't around to see my heroics. When Leo showed up at the park before the game, he told pitching coach Pete Reiser that he wasn't feeling well and might only stay an inning or two. He left after the 3rd inning, telling Pete to "Run it anyway you want." But Durocher didn't go home to recover from his illness; instead, he went to Chicago's downtown airport, Meigs Field, and got on a private plane to northern Wisconsin. From there Durocher attended parents' weekend at Camp Ojibway for his stepson, Joel Goldblatt, son of Lynne Walker Goldblatt, whom Leo had married just five weeks earlier. Not only that, he missed the next game against the Dodgers as well, which really ticked off Cubs owner P.K. Wrigley, who reportedly asked Herman Franks, a longtime associate of Durocher from his days with the New York Giants, to take over the Cubs on the spot. Herman was a clone of Leo in many ways, the same kind of in-your-face coaching style, but he told Wrigley that a move like that would be too disruptive to the team at that point. When Leo got back to Chicago, he had a three-hour meeting with Wrigley and agreed to "step aside" from his coaching duties with the Cubs. Whitey Lockman, who had been a director of player development, took over the helm, and we promptly won 39 of 65 games and moved up two places in the standings to finish the season in second place, 11 games back in the NL East, to the Pirates (who lost the NLCS to the Reds, who then went on to lose the World Series to the Oakland Athletics).

The Leo Durocher era had skidded to a halt in mid-season.

Durocher strategy meeting on the mound—1969

****

In his 7½ seasons at the helm of the Cubs, Leo racked up a 535–526 W/L record, gave the club its first winning season since 1945, and had us knocking on the door of playoff contention in 1969. His last season in baseball was 1973, when he retired after managing the Houston Astros. All of the four clubs he managed in his career had winning seasons, and he won a total of 2,008 games as a manager, including the 1954 World Series Champion, the New York Giants. Leo made a brief comeback in 1976 in the Japanese Pacific League with the Taiheiyo Club Lions, but he retired due to illness before the beginning of the season. As he signed off, Leo said, "Baseball has been 45 years of a wonderful life. But I have got a lot of things to do now. I'm going out to Palm Springs and I'm going to tee it up and play a lot of golf."

Durocher was fiery, caustic, vulgar, brilliant, and a fierce competitor. Even though he was relentless in his pressure on me behind the plate, we eventually found common ground and I began to understand a little bit of the method behind the madness. His 95 career game ejections ranks him fourth on the all-time list.

Leo Ernest Durocher passed away in 1991, at the age of 86. He was posthumously inducted into the National Baseball Hall of Fame in Cooperstown in 1994.

-8-
END OF THE LINE

In 1973 we came out of spring training like gangbusters with Whitey Lockman at the helm and, for the first half of the season, dominated the NL East. Not surprising because that stellar lineup that Cubs fans knew so well had remained intact, for the most part, through all the turmoil of the previous years. By its very nature, baseball is a game of failure, and if you get three hits out of ten, and can maintain that pace, you are a .300 hitter. But that's a number reserved for a very few. The game takes its toll in many ways, on and off the field. Losing is difficult, but can also galvanize a team together, which in turn can create long winning streaks. The usual suspects, Santo, Williams, Kessinger, and Beckert were on the roster, but in May of 1973, Joe Pepitone was traded to Atlanta for Andre Thornton. We added an infielder to the roster named Tony LaRussa, who played his final season of big-league ball with us after playing with Kansas City, Oakland, and the Braves. There was no way to know back then that Tony would go on to become one of the most successful managers in MLB history. For 33 years La Russa managed his teams to 3 World Series titles, 6 league championships, and 13 division titles. His total of 2,902 MLB wins as a manager is second only to the legendary Connie Mack's 3,731 victories. In 2013 Tony was elected to the Pro Baseball Hall of Fame by unanimous vote.

In baseball, you never know where a guy will end up.

Fergie still had his stuff on the mound and had just come off that '72 season celebrating his sixth consecutive season with 20 or more wins. We also had Milt "Gimpy" Pappas in rotation along with "Big Daddy" Rick Reuschel, Juan Pizarro, and Burt Hooton. Burt played with the Cubs until 1975, then was traded to LA, and became a household name in Los Angeles for his playoff appearances with the Dodgers. Burt had an All-Star game outing in 1981, and he was also named the NLCS MVP on the way to helping the Dodgers win a World Series and had four postseason wins in five game appearances.

Ernie Banks returned as a bench coach in 1973. Transitioning from one of the greatest to ever play the game to working the front office and being a bench coach wasn't easy, especially for a guy who wore the first number ever retired by the Chicago Cubs. However, Ernie was a stabilizing force as we battled for contention in the 102nd season of the franchise. Just having him on the bench where he had spent so many incredible seasons was important. His presence mattered and he was always keeping us up and moving forward.

****

By the end of June, we had a 47–31 record and 8½-game lead in the NL East. Once again, we were at the top of the division and then, just as we had in previous seasons, the bottom fell out and we dropped 33 out of 42 games, including losing 11 in a row in early August.

That streak knocked us out of the lead and below .500.

In June, Fergie made the announcement that he just didn't feel like playing baseball anymore, and after being one of the top pitchers in the game for so long, his words were understandable. It was an off-the-cuff comment and somewhat taken out of context, but nonetheless, it had the Cubs' faithful reeling at the announcement. Then on August 14th, there was the famous "bat-throwing incident" against the Braves at Wrigley. We'd lost nine in a row at that point, and after giving up five runs, Fergie was taken out of the game in the 5th inning by Whitey Lockman. During the pitching change, while Lockman, myself, some of the infielders, and home plate umpire Jerry Dale gathered on the mound waiting for Burt Hooton to come in from the bullpen, a baseball bat suddenly came flying out of the dugout toward home plate. Then a second, third, and fourth bat went airborne. Fergie was launching the Louisville Sluggers like toothpicks toward home plate. Obviously, Fergie wasn't very impressed with the balls and strikes that Dale had been calling and wanted him to know about it in no uncertain terms. When the press asked Fergie about the incident he said, "I thought the bat boy needed some extra work."

For Fergie, that loss would be his 12th of the season, and sixth out of seven starts. In a game with high stakes, it doesn't take much for the frustration to boil over, especially when you are a candidate for Cooperstown. It's an emotional game on every level, and the pressure on pitchers is intense. The wear and tear of throwing countless innings had taken a physical toll on Fergie, despite his Superman-like presence on the mound.

Baseball is a long season, and even though it's not a contact sport like football or hockey, it's a grueling game, especially for pitchers and catchers. Back in those days Fergie, and most of the other pitchers, would routinely go the distance in a nine-inning game. If there was the need for a relief pitcher, it was usually in the last inning or two. All the specialized pitchers in today's game had not yet been invented. After weeks of spring training, we would start playing ball in April, then the summer months would come along with the heat and humidity and nagging injuries, and then the season finally wrapped in September for most teams, as the playoffs went into October. That is a seven-month season, with all the travel, that also takes a bite out of your backside. Sleeping in hotels, grabbing buses, getting on planes, then after a few hours of sleep, adjusting your body clock to go from a day game at Wrigley to a slew of night games on the West Coast, and then trying to hit a round baseball with a round bat at 90 miles per hour could become a major challenge. I would routinely lose 10–15 pounds over the course of a season. Betty would cook me huge meals to help maintain my weight, health, and stamina, but often I had to pound down thick milkshakes to help me stabilize my weight.

Fergie eventually shook off his frustration for the game, but had a less-than-stellar year, ending up with a 14–15 W/L record and unusually high 3.89 ERA. Rick Monday who joined the team in the Holtzman trade in '71 cranked out 26 homers, Santo and Williams both hit 20 dingers, and José Cardenal added 11 round-trippers. José was traded to the Cubs in 1971 and led the team in batting with a .303 average as well as 33 doubles and 19 stolen bases. None of our other starters, Hooton, Reuschel, or Pappas, won more than 14 games—matter of fact, Milt also had a tough year, winning only 7 games and losing 12.

****

While the years have eroded much of that season, there was however one game that I remember well. On July 1st, we were playing a doubleheader against the Mets at Wrigley, and Koosman got the win while Fergie took the loss in game one. I had caught the first game and Whitey Lockman put Kenny Rudolph behind the plate for game two. We scored three runs on Mets' pitcher Harry Parker in the 1st, and eventually the Mets pushed in five runs on Larry Gura, and it stayed 5–3 into the bottom of the 9th. Tug McGraw was on the mound to close the game for NY, and José Cardenal led off with a single. Ronnie hit a gapper that put José on third with Ron on first. Pat Bourque was playing first base for us then, and he hit an infield grounder that got Cardenal trapped and tagged out. Then Santo was at second with Pat standing on first base, and it stayed that way as Paul Popovich flew out. Two outs followed, and the Wrigley Field fans were stomping their feet as Lockman pulled Rudolph and had me pinch-hit. McGraw's first pitch was a 90-mile-an-hour fastball right down the middle of the plate. I squared it up dead center on the barrel of my bat and hammered the ball into the deep seats in the left field bleachers for a two-out walk-off homer, which, considering the failure rate at the plate, is the greatest feeling in the game of baseball. Winning in such dramatic fashion is part of the game that makes up for all the one-run losses you endure over the course of a career.

While we weren't burning up the division, the truth is the rest of the NL East wasn't playing any better, and the division was nicknamed *"The National League Least."* On August 31st the Cardinals were in first place, just two games over .500, and the entire division was bound together by just a six-game spread, so basically it was all up for grabs.

On September 22nd we beat the Phillies 5–2 in 10 innings in Philadelphia and trailed the Mets by just 2½ games with eight games to go, but we were in fifth place. That's how close the race was. The Mets may have been in first place, but they were only one game over .500 at 78–77. It seemed like no team wanted to win the division, and it would make for an interesting end-of-the-season "battle of mediocrity" with all the teams hovering around .500 ball.

We went on to lose three of our next four games and sat right on the edge of mathematical elimination. But there were still four games to play against the Mets at Wrigley Field: single games Friday and Saturday and a doubleheader to end the season on Sunday, September 30th, due to a rainout from way back in May. As a matter of fact, 1973 was the only season between 1945 and 1984 in which the Cubs were still in contention to win the division on the very last day of the season.

Incredibly, both the Friday and Saturday games were rained out, so we were basically forced into back-to-back doubleheaders against the Mets on Sunday and Monday, the day after the regular season ended. We would need to win all four games in order to stay in contention for the postseason. We won the first game 1–0, but the Mets hammered us in the second game of the doubleheader, and we lost 9–2.

We still had to play that make-up doubleheader and as I recall, the game started at 11 a.m. just to make sure we got it in because it got dark early and there weren't any lights at Wrigley in 1973. By then the Pirates and Expos had been eliminated and only the Cardinals remained at an even 81–81 record and could tie the Mets, but we needed to sweep the Mets in that October 1st doubleheader.

That didn't happen.

We lost the first game 6–4 *and just like that, our season was over.* No need for the second game. Milt Pappas was scheduled to pitch the second game and the cancellation cost him the chance for his 100th career win in the NL. He came up one victory short of joining Cy Young and Jim Bunning as the only pitchers to win at least 100 games in each of the American and National Leagues. The Mets would go on and beat the Reds for the NCLS, only to lose the World Series to the Oakland A's in seven games. After all of that, we ended up in fifth place behind the Expos, Pirates, and Cardinals and just above the last-place Phillies.

I wasn't behind the plate for that final home stand at Wrigley, as Kenny Rudolph was calling the signals. By the end of the season I was thinking about how much further this team could go, so filled with talent—*albeit aging talent.* I was able to play in 124 games that season, even though the knee injuries had really taken their toll on my presence behind the plate, especially when it came to throwing out runners attempting to steal. You gotta have all the parts working to even have a chance to get a guy out at second base, and my knees were a weak point in my stance—and the opposing teams knew it. I had a better year at the plate, hitting 10 home runs and knocking in 42 RBI, but it was hardly a banner year.

Ever since the Mets caught us in 1969, they had become our nemesis, even more so than the Cardinals. Also, there was no way of knowing that 1973 would be the last season all the boys who brought so much excitement to Chicago would be wearing Cubbie blue.

****

Fergie Jenkins, Glenn Beckert, and Ron Santo were all traded after the 1973 season. Fergie went to Texas (where he promptly won a career-high of 25 games for the Rangers and was named "Comeback Player of the Year") for Bill Madlock and Vic Harris. Beckert and Bobby Fenwick were sent to the Padres for Jerry Morales, and Ronnie went to the White Sox in exchange for Steve Stone, Steve Swisher, and Ken Frailing. The only names left from the great '69 team were me, Billy Williams, and Don Kessinger. Billy played one more season in 1974 and was traded to Oakland. He was the only one of us who ever had the chance to play postseason ball. Billy was in three games in the 1975 ALCS for the Oakland A's and went 0–7 at the plate. Don played two more years with the Cubs, and then was traded to the St. Louis Cardinals in 1975. He finished his career in 1978 with the White Sox, where he would become the last player-manager in AL history.

Then, it was my turn.

On December 6, 1973, while listening to the morning news on WGN Radio in Chicago, I found out that I was traded to the Minnesota Twins for catcher George Mitterwald. No one from the Cubs front office called to tell me about the trade. Getting traded in baseball is often inevitable, but the way it went down stung me like a foul tip to the heart. I cannot tell you how devastating it was for me. I deserved at least a phone call, and to hear it on the news seemed really bush league. But, despite how it went down, I also felt beholden to the Cubs because of those great years that I had the chance to be part of and the men who became brothers to me.

And just like that, the 1969 Cubs were no more. Not sure who hurt more, me or the fans who had supported us for so long, as they had become an integral part of the team. It was a great run, but nothing lasts forever, especially in baseball.

Connecting with a blind fan at Wrigley in 1969

I consoled myself thinking that at least I was still playing in the Midwest, even though it was the American League team. I'm not sure what I would have done if I had been traded to the Mets or Cardinals, or even been traded to the West Coast, so far from Betty and the kids. The upside was that Bill Hands was there waiting for me, having been dealt by the Cubs to the Twins after the 1972 season along with Joe Decker and Bob Maneely in exchange for Dave LaRoche. During the 1974 season Hands and I lived next door to each other, in log cabins, on Lake Minnetonka, and went to the park together each day. This arrangement reminded us of our early years with the Giants and great seasons with the Cubs. Spring training for the Twins was in Florida, a very different climate from the dry heat of the Cubs training facility in Arizona. Minneapolis stays a lot colder longer than Chicago, and adjusting wasn't easy for me.

In 1974 I only played in 32 games for the Twins after damaging my knee (again) in a scuffle at home plate on June 20th. I was able to catch a few innings in August that season, but my knee was in really bad shape. I consulted with my doctor in Chicago, and we decided that I should have one more knee surgery after the season was over. Post-op, I picked up a staph infection in the knee and a blood clot that almost took my life. I made it past the clot, but eventually, the infection exploded out of my knee during a workout. I will spare the gory details here, but suffice to say that by October of '74, I was taken off the Twins 40-man roster.

Man, that was a tough time, but with my family beside me, and my faith, I pushed through it all, as I always have.

I had given everything (and more) to the game, but nagging injuries were getting the better of me and in baseball terms, I was an old man at the age of 32, especially as a catcher. I never had the chance to move to first base, as some guys have, like Mike Piazza and Joe Maurer. Back then moving out from behind the plate rarely happened, and the move might have saved my knees, but I'd be out of the business of calling pitches, and that was my thing.

Betty, Julie, Renee, and Todd

After the offseason knee surgery and the infection cleared up, I went to Arizona and worked out with the legendary powerlifter Jon Cole to rehab my knee. I got to the point where I was squatting with 500 pounds and, in some ways, was in the best shape of my life. Jon pushed me from one end of the gym to the other, and I was ready to give baseball one more shot. In April of 1975, the San Diego Padres signed me as a free agent after inviting me to spring training. I managed to play in 74 games for the Padres that year, even though my primary role was to work with the young pitching staff, improving them greatly with my presence and experience. After that season, the Padres released me, but also offered to have me be a player-coach with Hawaii in the Pacific League, but I turned it down. I wasn't quite ready to hang up the cleats.

Oddly enough, I began talking with the Cubs, and two years after they let me go, I got an offer to rejoin the team that meant so much to me. On April 13, 1976, I signed on for the second time in my career with the Chicago Cubs and was heading back to "The Friendly Confines" one more time. As I said, when it comes to baseball, you never know where you will end up.

Behind the plate with the Padres

-9-
RETURN TO WRIGLEY

On the second day of the 1976 season, I once again found myself in the batter's box at Wrigley Field on a beautiful sun-washed spring afternoon. This time I was facing Mets reliever Bob Apodaca in the bottom of the 7th inning. The big green scoreboard in center field showed the Cubs down 5–3 after Mets slugger Dave "Kong" Kingman parked one on Waveland Avenue for two runs. I'd relieved Steve Swisher behind the plate in the top of the inning and had a "*good to see ya*" pat on the back from home-plate ump Dutch Rennert. I dug into the dirt in the box, and on the very first pitch, I took the ball deep into the gap in right-center and, without too much difficulty, found myself standing on second base as the fans roared their approval.

I had a serious emotional moment, right then and there, and it's an image frozen forever in my mind. The applause and shouts from the fans washed over me, and I just hung my head down in a prayer of thanks to the Lord for letting me play baseball back in Chicago, one more time.

I could see the guys on the bench all standing up and clapping as well, and I think a couple of Mets players even joined in. It was an extremely powerful experience for me, one that stands out among so many great times in my career. I'd never thought I would be back in a Cubs uniform after I was traded, and yet there I was, smack-dab in the middle of the place that meant the world to me for so many years. All the hard work, surgeries, travel, trades, and faith had once again paid off.

The double I hit sparked a Cubs rally, and we beat the Mets 6–5. Anytime we could take out the team that caught us in '69 was always a great victory.

I made it about a month into the season before the benches cleared with the Giants on May 1st, and during the scrum, I stretched a muscle in my shoulder. I ended up on the 15-day DL and underwent surgery to remove a disc and fuse two connecting vertebrae in my neck on June 15th. That was basically the end of my comeback year with the Cubs, as I only played in 13 games, but there are a couple of games that really stand out from that 1976 season.

****

On April 17th, the Phillies were in Wrigley for our first series of the season. Philadelphia had Steve Carlton on the mound; we had "Big Daddy" Rick Reuschel throwing for us. The Phillies were loaded with talent, with Garry Maddox, Dick Allen, Larry Bowa, Dave Cash, Jay Johnstone, Greg "the Bull" Luzinski, and super-slugger Mike Schmidt on the roster. By the bottom of the 3rd inning, we had a comfortable early lead and were on top 11–1, which included homers from Monday and Swisher. By the 5th inning, we were rolling along at 13–2, but you can't ever put a game in the win column until after the final out. Mike Schmidt would have an incredible day at the plate, hitting four out of the nine home runs, and we proceeded to blow a 13–2 lead, losing 18–16 when Mike hit his fourth dinger in the 10th inning. It was a home-run slugfest for the records books.

At one point, I thought the home-plate ump was going to run out of baseballs.

One week later, we were at Dodger Stadium on April 25th playing a tough LA team. In the bottom of the 4th inning, lead-off hitter Ted Sizemore was at the plate for the Dodgers, and Ken Crosby was on the mound for the Cubs. All of a sudden, there were two fans in the outfield kneeling down over something on the ground, trying to light a match. I can remember Tommy Lasorda running as fast as his short legs would take him toward the two, cursing like a sailor who had just lost his shore leave. I was watching from the dugout, getting ready to sprint to the outfield, when the next thing I knew, here came Rick Monday from his position in center field, and in one scoop, he grabbed an American flag off the ground, that had been doused with lighter fluid. This guy (and, as it turned out, his 11-year-old son) were attempting to burn Old Glory at Dodger Stadium.

In quick order, the culprits were apprehended, and Monday handed the flag to Dodger pitcher Doug Rau. Shortly thereafter the left field message board lit up with *"Rick Monday ... You Made A Great Play."* Then the crowd at Dodger Stadium broke out into a spontaneous chorus of "God Bless America." It was a scene I will never forget. That day at Dodger Stadium still makes the news all these years later.

Rick Monday was a US Marine Corps reservist, and trying to burn a flag in front of him was absolutely the wrong plan. While the official end of the Vietnam War was in 1975, a lingering sentiment of anti-war protesters remained, and while I don't know what this guy and his kid were trying to prove, Rick's actions that day became the stuff of legend, especially in 1976, the bicentennial year of America. In some sort of perfect baseball karma after that season, Rick (who had a great year, batting .272 with 32 home runs and 77 RBI) and pitcher Mike Garvin were traded from the Cubs to the Dodgers for Bill Buckner and Ivan DeJesus. Rick played with the Dodgers from 1977 to 1984, and his biggest highlight was a tie-breaking ninth-inning home run in the pivotal Game 5 of the 1981 NL Championship Series at Montreal that gave Los Angeles a 2–1 victory over the Expos. If that's not enough, he went into the Dodgers broadcast booth after he retired and the two-time All-Star is in his 31st season as a Dodger broadcaster and 39th season overall with the organization, including 8 as a player.

Rick was an excellent baseball player and is a great broadcaster, and his actions that day back in 1976, on some level, was a statement that many Americans could relate to. The Baseball Hall of Fame named Monday's act as one of the 100 Classic Moments in the history of the game.

I watched the rest of the 1976 season from the dugout because, at that point, the Cubs had four healthy catchers on the roster. Steve Swisher had come over from the White Sox in the Santo trade in '73 and had been handling the bulk of the catching duties. George Mitterwald, Ed Putman, and Tim Hosley filled in behind Swisher. Steve wore my old #9, and after wearing that number for so many seasons, it was a sign, of sorts, that my time as a major league ballplayer was coming to an end. The upside was that after so many years of being behind the plate, I had the opportunity to see the game from a different angle and perspective. I knew when my playing days were over that I'd be interested in coaching. My deep background in handling pitchers from behind the dish, the years with Durocher, and being the field general—all those experiences had rubbed off on me in a big way.

We finished in fourth place in the division, 26 games behind the division-winning Phillies, who had a great year at 101–61, but lost to Cincinnati in the NLCS 3–0. Mike Schmidt, who started that bombing raid back in April at Wrigley, won the first of his 10 Gold Gloves that year, and batted .308 during the series against the Reds, who also had an incredible season (nearly identical to the Phillies), 102–60. The Reds hammered the Yankees into submission, winning four straight games to claim the World Series title in 1976. That offseason, more changes happened for the Cubs organization, on and off the field.

****

In November, Bob Kennedy was named head of baseball operations. His first directive was to inform Jim Marshall that he was fired as manager. Marshall had taken over for Whitey Lockman in the middle of the 1974 season, after a dismal first half. In desperation, P.K. Wrigley actually reached out to Leo Durocher and asked him to return as manager for the 1977 season, but Leo turned him down. Herman Franks, who had a short stint as a Cubs coach under Durocher, was named the new manager. I knew Herman back from my days with the Giants (even though he never really was behind me with the whole one-handed catching style) and I hoped to find some new direction with the Cubs when he was named manager.

It didn't take long for the direction to show itself. In December of 1976, Herman named me bullpen coach and emergency back-up catcher. This was the last step in my time as a player, and the first toward whatever lay ahead in my post-playing days. Becoming a coach seemed to be the natural progression of my pro baseball career.

That 1977 season was another one for the record books, for all the wrong reasons. By June we experienced our usual strong early season start and were up 8½ games over the Phillies. By All-Star break, we were only up 2 games over Philly, as we were 19 games over .500 and feeling good about all phases of the game. Once again the bottom dropped out and we went 20–40 and finished the season in fourth place with an 81–81 record.

With all my years in baseball, I've never been able to quite pin-point what makes or breaks a season for a particular team. There are some indicators that are more obvious, like Durocher playing his starters to the point of exhaustion in '69 while the Mets platooned their players, keeping them fresh. Injuries play a role, especially when it comes to key personnel and the unavoidable wear and tear during the season, but it's also a mental battle. When you are winning (like we did in 1969 with 155 days in first place), you feel untouchable, like you can do no wrong. The confidence that comes with that type of winning is infectious. However, all it takes is one ball that gets through the infield, a called *ball four*, instead of *strike three*, errors that seem to come out of nowhere, or some batter hits a walk-off dinger and you lose in the bottom of the 9th. Winning is a habit, and so is losing to the same degree. Batting slumps are part of the game, and overthinking every pitch in an attempt to get out of the hole once you've gone 0–18 at the plate is when your mind starts to really mess with you.

I never worried too much about my batting average, but I did have a terrible experience with the "*yips*," which are a sudden and unexplained loss of athletic skills in experienced athletes caused by a mental short-circuit. This is when an infielder loses the ability to make a routine play or a catcher struggles to throw the ball back to the pitcher, which is exactly what happened to me in my first year under Leo Durocher.

****

We'd just had another chewing-out in the clubhouse during spring training, and Leo said to all of us in no uncertain terms, "If you can't play for me, I will damn sure find someone to take your place!" and I think mentally I somehow took a hit, and it showed up in my throwing arm. The next game I went out to warm up in the bullpen, where two pitchers and two catchers are really close to each other, but all of a sudden, I couldn't throw the bloomin' ball back to the guy I was warming up! There was a total disconnect from what my mind wanted me to do and my body responding to the orders given. I bounced them back, threw one or two over the pitcher's head, and almost hit the guy next to him a few times. All I kept thinking was that I was done with my MLB career before it even started, because once Leo found out that his catcher couldn't throw the ball back to the mound, much less take down a runner trying to steal second base, I would be back in Virginia working construction with my dad.

The term "yips" is attributed to Tommy Armour, a golf champion and later golf teacher, to explain the difficulties that led him to quit tournament play. In describing the yips, golfers have used terms like jitters and jerks as their game unravels. Matter of fact, researchers at the Mayo Clinic found that 33% to 48% of all serious golfers have experienced the yips. Well, I don't know if the folks at Mayo studied baseball players, but I can tell you it's a scary thing. One moment you are in control of your faculties and performance, and the next thing you know, you can hardly roll a ball back to the guy who threw it to you. One of the most well-known cases of the yips is Steve Blass, an All-Star pitcher for the Pirates from 1964 to 1974. In a 10-season major league career, Blass posted a 103–76 record with 896 strikeouts and a 3.63 ERA in 1,597 innings pitched, including 16 shutouts and 57 complete games. And then, an unexplained loss of pitching control after the 1972 season. His ERA soared to 9.85 in the 1973 season, during which he walked 84 batters in 88 $\frac{2}{3}$ innings, and struck out only 27.

Over the years, I faced Steve more than a few times in my career, and to see this guy who was an incredible force on the mound simply "lose his stuff" almost overnight was frightening.

I had to figure out a way out of the hole. I went to a hypnotist a few times, but that didn't work. I did some work on my physical mechanics, but that didn't help either, and my frustration increased. One day I read an article about a book called *Psycho-Cybernetics* by Maxwell Maltz, which included the concept of "visualization" when it came to one's goals. My only goal at that point was to get the ball out of my mitt and throw it 60 feet, 6 inches back to the pitcher on the mound. I bought the book and followed Maltz's instructions, which included "seeing myself" throwing that ball back to the mound with ease, as I had done a thousand times before.

Incredibly, after a few sessions, my body began to respond and the uplink between my mind and throwing arm was reestablished. I have to say that I always worried that it might happen again, but luckily it didn't. If Leo ever noticed something was off, he never mentioned it. On a side note, I imparted those techniques to my kids back when Todd was playing baseball and hockey, Renee was in track, and Chad was playing both football and baseball. Much like my dad did for me, I rarely missed any of their high school games or track meets.

In 1977 I played in just two games and went 0–4 at the plate, and on October 12th I was released from the Cubs for the second time in my career.

This time, it wasn't a surprise, and I got to finish my playing career with the Chicago Cubs.

In 14 seasons, I played in 1,061 games and 8,847 innings, racked up 813 hits in 3,442 at-bats for a .236 career batting average along with 82 home runs, 381 runs batted in with a .292 on-base percentage, and a .9903 fielding percentage. That ranks me 111th out of the top 375 catchers in MLB fielding history, and right behind the current Chicago Cubs manager, David Ross, who had a .9904 fielding percentage in 15 seasons and caught 5,991 innings.

I had been a part of some great teams and had gained a ton of experience, but my playing days were over. I still wanted to stay in the game and manage in order to help develop ball clubs into winners.

It wasn't long before I had my chance.

With Rick Monday—1977

-10-
GAME OVER

You can't play baseball forever, but coaching can extend your baseball life, and that's what I wanted to do when my time behind the plate ended. When Herman Franks installed me as the bullpen coach, it was my first step toward a coaching career that I hoped would land me as the manager of a big-league team. I was Herman's right-hand man and learned a lot of what coaching was all about from him, and I knew that all those years behind the plate, as well as the seasons with Durocher, made me a natural to eventually manage a big-league ball club.

In 1978, my first coaching experience after my playing days was in Bradenton, Florida, where I was given the opportunity to manage the Cubs rookie league team. I did pretty well that first season, and then in 1979 I was promoted to manager of the Cubs Double-A affiliate in Midland, Texas, which at that time was in the middle of nowhere. The surroundings and accommodations were a far cry from what I had grown used to in the majors, but I knew even with my background and accomplishments, I had to pay my dues in order to become a manager. I got to know the state of Texas very well with all the road games and saw way more horned toads than can easily be counted, and during my two years in Midland, the team won one division title and nearly won another.

But in baseball, *almost* doesn't count for much.

In 1981 I was named the manager of the Cubs Triple-A club in Des Moines, Iowa, the Iowa Oaks. At that point, I was literally one rung down on the baseball ladder from my goal of coaching in the big leagues. Unfortunately, we got off to a horrible start, and the Iowa Oaks were sitting at 12–30 in the W/L column when the Cubs Director of Player Development, C.V. Davis, reached out to me. He knew we were struggling and promised me that he was going to get some new players for the team, who I could develop and work with, in order to turn the season around. This opportunity would keep me moving upward in the pipeline for managing.

But that's not how it turned out.

One night on a road trip, he called me down to his room, and instead of telling me had a crop of new players, C.V. began to tell me that there needed to be a complete overhaul, including the manager position, and that eventually, he'd figure out a place for me in the organization. In effect, I was being fired right then and there.

To say I was stunned would be putting it mildly.

I quietly said, "Do what you have to do," and left the room. I went back to my hotel room and called Betty in Chicago. I said, "Baby, I've just been fired." She didn't take it as easily as I had and said, "Randy, you've earned the right to manage and to be treated fairly by the Cubs. Now go back and tell him exactly what you think about this!"

Betty was right, I deserved better.

I bulldozed my way back to C.V.'s room, hammered on the door, and proceeded to tell him in no uncertain terms that he could take the job and shove it up his fanny (multiple times as I recall). I really read the riot act to him because on some level, I knew that my chances of making it back to the majors were being taken away from me, and I had no control over the decision. It was a sinking feeling, to say the least. My entire career was slowly going down the drain, and there was seemingly nothing I could do to stop it.

I called Betty back, and we prayed together over the phone about what had just happened. We talked about it at length, and deep down I knew that my time with the Cubs organization was over. I'd given my all to the team, a lot of blood, sweat, more than a few tears, and the firing was a real gut punch. To top it all off, it was my 39th birthday, and I thought about how, when I had returned to my 10th high school reunion in 1970, I was a major league catcher, and I had hoped that by the 20th reunion, I'd be a big-league manager, but that wasn't going to happen. I worked hard my entire career and believing I somehow came up short didn't sit well with me. Unfortunately for me, C.V. Davis's decision sealed my fate as far as my big-league baseball future.

The next day I packed my bags and headed back to Chicago. I spent some time trying to regain my bearings, trying to figure out what I was going to do as a career because, at that point, it looked like baseball was over for me.

Even so, I went to the winter meetings looking for a coaching job, met with a few minor league teams, and after just a couple of days, I knew there was no way I could put up with the B.S. that goes into much of the game at that level. So, there I was, an unemployed Gold Glove–winning All-Star player, and one of the most recognized Cubs to ever wear the uniform, and I needed to find a job. Baseball was all I ever knew, and outside of the offseason jobs I took to make ends meet, I really wasn't trained for anything else. However, I did find a job as an investment banker, which is something I had done in the offseason years before, and that helped to keep my mind off my former glory days.

As it turned out, not having a major league managing career was a blessing in disguise. God had other plans for my talent and passion for baseball that would create a much more profound experience for me and thousands of fans. A plan beyond just working with players in the big leagues, babysitting egos, worrying about lineup cards, and the endless treadmill of a major league baseball season.

****

One day in 1982, my neighbor approached me with the idea of setting up baseball camps for kids at Harper College, located not far from our home. After some thought on the idea, I approached the athletic director at the college, and he readily agreed to rent out their facility for camps. In no time at all, the camps became a success and really took off. We had hundreds of young ballplayers sign up to learn the basic skills of the game. On one hand, it was far more satisfying to work with the young kids rather than some of the minor league talent who were striving to make a major league club, because the kids were playing for the love of the game. Every time I held an instructional camp, the young players took me back to my early days in baseball, and after so many years dealing with Durocher, the Mets, a black cat, injuries, C.V. Davis, and all the rest, my love for the game was slowly being replenished. That's not to say that it wasn't a grind of a different sort, and the weekly outings took a toll on my hillbilly fanny, but I loved it.

Looking for some added support, I asked my friend Rich Melman, the founder of the *Lettuce Entertain You* restaurants, if he would come out to the camp and speak to the kids about persistence, something Rich knows a great deal about. As a kid, he sold ice cream and peanuts on the beaches in Chicago and even sold eggs door to door, a tough way to make a buck. At 14, he started working for the family restaurant business but soon broke off on his own. Eventually, he connected with the late realty guru Jerry Orzoff, who believed in Rich's talent, and they became a formidable tag team in business. Fast-forward to 1988, and *Lettuce Entertain You* had 27 restaurants and was bringing in about $90 million a year. Not bad for a guy who had three unsuccessful attempts at college. The company was guided by a philosophy based on the importance of partnership, sharing responsibilities and ideas, developing and growing together, with a "culture of caring" that has been essential to the company since day one. Those same ingredients are needed to create a winning team in baseball and have been the guide post for Melman's incredible success.

Not long after one of Rich's appearances, we went out to dinner. By that point, I had a partner working with me on the kids camps who joined us. After eating, we talked as we walked back to our cars, and Rich blurted out, "Randy, why don't you do a baseball camp for adults?" My partner jumped in with, "Hey, can you get some former players to come out to the college for an adult camp?" I thought about it for a moment, and then the idea hit me, square between the eyes.

"Nope. What I can do is get some field time at the Cubs facilities in Arizona, with some of my old teammates participating, and have the camp be like spring training."

That was the moment the fantasy camp idea was born.

When I was in high school, I used to read about all the big-leaguers going to spring training and thought that it was really unfair that grown men got paid to go to Florida and Arizona to play baseball. Of course, it didn't seem unfair to me when I participated in spring training nearly two dozen times as a major league catcher and as a coach and minor league manager. Spring training is a rite of passage, it's the first step back to America's pastime, and I always counted down the days when pitchers and catchers would report before any of the other players. There was something that would happen to me, almost a sense of hope and renewal, when I would squat down behind the plate in Arizona to start taking pitches from Fergie and the guys. The aches and pains of the past season, as well as the winter months, would fade away, and the promise of warmth and Opening Day beckoned.

If I could recreate that spring training experience for baseball fans, it would be as close as they could get to the experience of being a big-league ball player. I also knew that a lot of my former teammates would really enjoy putting on a uniform once again and participating in the experience.

At that time, there was no such thing as a "fantasy camp," outside of some corporate events that teams put on as a meet-and-greet for their clients to hang out with former ballplayers. What I was going for was a way for diehard baseball fans to suit up and hang with their heroes. There was no business model to follow so I created one, just as if I was building my own baseball organization, because on many levels it was just that. We'd need marketing, public relations, facility management, player management, financing, equipment, and all of the other things that go into a baseball club. I started to float the idea to some of my former teammates and the response was a serious thumbs up. However, there were a handful of guys who didn't really know what to make of my plans, and I got a few "if it really happens, call me" responses as well.

So, I began to sketch out and build the camp concept on a legal pad right on our kitchen table. Betty was all for it, even though there was much uncertainty about the idea, but once again we offered it up in prayer. We had so many questions that didn't yet have answers. Could I secure the needed connection and contacts with the Cubs, the team that had fired me as manager? Would they even be interested in some sort of partnership with me? Would Cubs fans buy into the idea? Could I keep a rotating roster of former major league players to make it work? What about logistics? How should the camp experience be designed? How many times a year? What would it cost? Most importantly for me, could I create a business model that provided income for my family? Those questions, and a million more, weighed on my mind.

I decided to brand the experience as *"The place where lifelong dreams come true"* and aimed the idea at adults 30+ years of age. Back then, I figured that age group would have the most connection to the 1969 Cubs, and that would be my sweet spot for promoting the idea. Plus, I didn't want some 20-year-old signing up to try and impress the former big-leaguers in an attempt to make a name for themselves. We had to under-promise and over-deliver the big-league experience if the thing had any chance of making it long term. I decided that each rookie or "camper" would receive a package that included an authentic, personalized Cubs uniform, a baseball card with their picture on the front and stats on the back, a "million-dollar" contract, all the needed equipment, and a videotape of the big game against the former Cubs players on the final day of camp.

But the biggest selling point was the accessibility to former players, both on and off the field. We were not just offering a chance to play baseball in a Cubs uniform, we were creating the opportunity for fans to have the most authentic experience of being a major league ball player possible, and that meant being coached by some of my former teammates, even playing a game against some great Chicago Cubs stars. We were literally breaking down the unseen barrier between the fans and the players and allowing the two to merge, in a way that had never been done before.

It was an exhilarating, scary, and daunting task all at the same time.

After locking down the concept and securing the facilities in Arizona (and later at the University of Chicago and Wrigley Field), I used my local media contacts to set up a few interviews about the idea, and word started to spread. Fans were curious about this new camp that would put them on the same playing field as Ron Santo, Ernie Banks, and Fergie Jenkins. They began to wonder what it would be like to spend a week in Arizona, in the sunshine, shagging fly balls, running sprints, taking batting practice, and then hanging out at the pool after practice with the likes of Don Kessinger, Glenn Beckert, and Gene Oliver.

In late 1982, the momentum grew, and fans started to sign up, plunking down $2,195 to attend a week-long fantasy camp experience. Then, in January of 1983, we had our first crop of campers ready to go, and "Randy Hundley's Baseball Fantasy Camp" was open for business.

It took a few years for me to see it, but in hindsight, C.V. Davis did me a favor.

-11-
FIELD OF DREAMS

So, there I was in the middle of January in beautiful Scottsdale, Arizona, at Indian School Field. In front of me stood 63 rookie campers, who were all eager to play ball. They were wearing official Cubs uniforms, with their number and name on the back of their jersey. They had brought their own mitts and gloves, and while they were middle aged on paper, in their hearts they were the boys (and later the girls) of summer once again. Mixed in with the novices were a few ringers, guys who had played high school or college baseball, and many of them had spent a couple of months getting ready for the camp. Running, lifting weights, trying to lose a few pounds, and working out muscles that had long been dormant.

In setting up that inaugural camp, I knew we had to have a fitness component, so I brought on a marathon runner to come in to lead the stretching and warm-up prior to the campers starting drills for the day. I didn't want any pulled hamstrings every single morning during calisthenics, but that didn't prevent a camper from being injured during fielding drills. Right out of the gate, a camper got hurt when a ground ball he was trying to catch had a crazy bounce and caught him in the knee.

He ended up rolling around on the ground in pain and had to be taken off the field on a cart, just like a big-leaguer! Of course, in the stands was a full cadre of reporters, who had made the stop in Arizona on their way to the Super Bowl in Pasadena. They had started interviewing me about this new "fantasy camp" idea and jumped all over the fact that some guy got hurt before a game was even played. "You guys couldn't wait to see this, could ya?" I barked at the reporters. However, as so many times in my career, it turned out to be another blessing in disguise. Our hero ended up having surgery, and after a couple of recovery days, he was back on the field, with crutches and wearing his uniform. The reporters were all over his story, which gave us some serious free PR.

Another moment that stands out from that first camp is with a psychiatrist named Dr. Harry Soloway. He had called three times wanting to join in, but always found an excuse to bow out. After my third call with the guy, I came to find out that he felt he'd be embarrassed because he had never played organized baseball. I reminded him that his career choice included getting people to go past their fears and self-imposed boundaries, which sort of put him on the spot. He relented, came to camp, and in the course of things, became somewhat of a local celebrity in Scottsdale, which of course brought out the journalists. One of them wrote in the local paper that the guy was "*the worst baseball player he'd ever seen, on any field, anywhere, including sandlot ball.*" When the shrink-turned-ballplayer read the article, he was incensed and said that he'd never would grant another interview, ever!

That's when I told him he was really a major leaguer!

But the story doesn't end there.

During an intrasquad game later in the week, I pinch-hit with the bases loaded and two outs. I hit a monster shot which rocketed high up and right toward Dr. Harry, who was in deep left field. He started running in circles under it as I was yelling at him to stay put under the ball. After going back and forth, he stuck out his glove, and incredibly, the ball landed smack-dab in the pocket! It was just like the movie *The Sandlot* when the kid closes his eyes and the ball finds its way into his glove! The look on his face remains with me to this day. He had overcome his fears and was so proud to catch that ball. A moment like that can change a life. Amazingly, Dr. Harry attended three more camps. For over 30 years, I've watched grown men and women become kids again, right in front of my eyes. After the success of that first camp, I immediately planned a second camp in Scottsdale, just two months later, in April, and it quickly filled up.

****

The big shift came when I was able to talk Leo Durocher into coaching many of his former Cubs players and convinced Charlie Grimm and Cy Young–winning pitcher Steve Stone to be the managers for the team of rookies in the second camp. Even though there was no pennant at stake, watching Leo yell at his former players was well worth the price of admission. My battery mate, Ferguson Jenkins, was at that second camp as well. He was the only active player, as Fergie would go on to retire after the 1983 season with the Cubs. Glenn Beckert dropped what he was doing as a commodities trader to patrol the infield, and "Gentleman" Jim Hickman took a break from his farm to give instruction at first base, just like Ron Santo did over at third. Gene Oliver, Billy Williams, Rich Nye, and Ernie Banks were all in Cubbie blue once again. Every one of them coached and played for expenses only.

That second camp concluded with a 15-inning game and the Cubs pros (managed by Durocher) beat the campers/rookies (managed by Grimm and Stone) by a score of 23–6. Everyone involved had one heck of a great time. But the most memorable moment came when tough-as-nails Leo Durocher stood up at the banquet the night after the big game and, in a halting voice, apologized to Ron Santo for his comments around the whole "Ron Santo Day" clubhouse incident that took place a full 13 years earlier in 1969. All of us who played for Leo sat there with our mouths hanging open, not believing what we were hearing. The emotion in the room was incredible and to watch Ronnie go up and embrace Leo was something I never thought I'd see. One by one, Leo Durocher's former players went up to shake his hand or give him a hug, and there were a few tears as well.

The campers knew they were witnesses to a rare moment.

The stories and memories from the years that we ran camp are inspiring, heart-warming, hilarious, and profound. Over the years, I've received a bat bag full of letters about the fantasy camp experience, and I take great pride in sharing some of them here.

Leading off is Beth Chaplin…

I've been a die-hard Cubs fan since the age of 4. I was particularly attached to the 1969 and the 1984 teams. I don't remember the first time I learned of the Cubs Fantasy Camps, but I immediately wanted to attend. I never thought I'd be able to go. Many years later, I received my spot on the roster for my 40th birthday. I was excited and quite nervous. I wanted to play baseball and get autographs for a once-in-a-lifetime experience. As it turned out, it was all that—and much more.

Fergie Jenkins and Carmen Fanzone were my coaches for my first camp. I got my first hit—a line drive to right field. When Hall of Famer Ferguson Jenkins gave me a high five and said, "nice hit, young lady," I was so glad I was wearing sunglasses to hide the tears in my eyes. It was a pinch-me moment. (There would be many more such moments!)

I've played baseball at the Cubs Fantasy Camp 13 times, from 2003 to 2020. The highlight memory is when my dad joined me for one of those camps. We were the first father/daughter pair to ever attend camp. It was a thrill—especially when Dad hit a double with me at first. Rick Reuschel waved me around third to score on Dad's double! That was a sweet RBI and a fantastic moment!

Randy, your brilliant vision of a pro sports baseball camp has given us the experience of being a pro (although without the talent of pro players), but I'm not sure even you could have anticipated the friendships, connections, and joy that would ripple far beyond the camp. I'm so grateful to you for creating some of the finest experiences of my life!

Beth Chaplin, Fergie Jenkins, and David Chaplin

And this from Eddy Piper...

Imagine you are told that by the time you're 65, you will probably be in a wheelchair because you have an incurable disease! How would you react? Most of us will probably start thinking about things we wish we had done when we were healthy. For me—it was baseball. I always had a fantasy when I was younger that I was playing for the Chicago Cubs.

Oh, how I wished I could have a chance to play a few ballgames at the Cubs training facility! But there was an obstacle to playing with Parkinson's disease. I could see my deterioration in throwing, hitting, and catching. I had to create some sort of temporary nerve override to function despite the extreme pain and stiffness.

Randy, I will never forget when I entered the Cubs locker room and you told me I could play! You knew about my situation and again pledged to give me 100 percent support to allow me to fulfill my dream of being a Cubs player! You had me so pumped during the first baseball camp that I returned a second time the following year to try again. You met me with great enthusiasm at the second fantasy camp and spent considerable time with me at the batting cage trying to go over the basics of hitting while giving me a new stance to compensate for the limitations placed on me by Parkinson's disease.

I was so nervous in the last game we played. As I got up to bat I tried to remember everything you taught me. I fouled off the ball seven times and eventually got a single! I'll never forget the way the crowd cheered and how the umpire gave me the game ball. The next batter drove me home with a double RBI, and as I ran to home, there you were at home plate, hugging me, shaking my hand, and congratulating me on getting a hit. It was indeed a dream come true. Thank you, Randy!

Bob Farinelli remembers his experience at the camp...

Randy, for my 40th birthday I decided to fulfill my dream of attending your camp. I filled out an application and sent it in. A few weeks later, the phone rang. My wife Cathy answered, and said to me, "It's for you, he says he's Randy Hundley." What a thrill it was, to speak with the great Cubs catcher personally, and to hear you say, "You made the roster!"

At my first camp, I wasn't very good. I hadn't played baseball in over 25 years. My coaches were Fergie Jenkins and Gene Oliver. Spending time talking baseball with them was incredible! I went home from my "once-in-a-lifetime" experience sore and tired. The week in Arizona far surpassed my expectations.

The following summer my family and I attended an Iowa Cubs game in Des Moines. Wandering around the concourse, we came upon a table where Fergie was sitting, signing autographs. I walked over and to my surprise, Fergie said, "Hey, Bob, are we going to see you again next year?" Cathy and I were stunned that Fergie remembered me. Cathy looked at me and said, "If Fergie wants you to go back, I guess you have to go."

As of this letter, I have attended 19 consecutive camps. The streak ended with the cancellation due to Covid-19 in 2021. Over the years I found myself working to stay in reasonable shape all year long, in preparation for the next camp. Most of my friends are fellow campers. At the camp, all the people involved develop a special bond that is truly remarkable. Randy, you've created something very special, and the camp regulars and the coaches have become a cohesive baseball family.

At one camp, I had a long at-bat against Ron Davis. This was during the "Big Game" where the campers play an inning and get an at-bat against the former major leaguers. I kept fouling pitches off and you would say, "Nice swing, you're right on it." Eventually, I swung and missed what I thought was a splitter. After the game, you made it a point to find me and said, "I hope you know you shouldn't be disappointed. That was a great at-bat. Ron had to throw a heck of a pitch to get you."

Randy, that may or may not be true, but when you said it, I believed it. Your generosity and that of the coaches was amazing. They shared wisdom and wonderful stories of their lives in baseball. Randy, because of you, many thousands of baseball lovers have had the opportunity to enjoy this experience and become members of a new baseball family. I know that for me and other members of my Cubs baseball family, your camp has become part of our identities.

Matt Veto shares his memories ...

What I remember most is that our father smiled for six straight days, and his three sons smiled with him. At 71 years old, in 2014, Dad was perhaps slightly past his prime ball-playing days. The jersey was snug. His feet were sluggish. But the pinnacle of his athletic career — of all of our careers — came during six spring days in Mesa, Arizona, when the four of us pretended to play for the Chicago Cubs. It felt so real ... and surreal. The Cubs logo on our chest. Our names on our backs. The pinstripes. This is how we looked as we stepped to the plate in our imagination. But here we were, the sun beating on our backs, trotting to our positions in the Sloan Park outfield. My brothers and I were familiar with these spots on the diamond. The outfield grass was our summer home as kids and young adults. But being there together with our father to complete the "Veto outfield" forged a powerfully permanent memory. During the camp, my older brother Jim hit two home runs. My oldest brother, Jason, frequently doubled to the gap. But our father—Jim "Papa V" Veto—was the star, doted on by our fantasy teammates and our coaches, Lee Smith and Pete LaCock. "It was an amazing opportunity to share something all four of us loved with equal enthusiasm," my dad said. "It was a dream."

The Veto Boys

Another memory from Jerry Gaul...

My father, Jerry, met Randy through a mutual business connection the summer after Randy ran his first Cubs Fantasy Camp the previous January in Mesa, Arizona. The mutual business connection was at The Hamilton Hotel in Itasca, Illinois. It was a July 4th celebration and Randy and former Cubs players and campers from that first camp were playing an exhibition game there. Randy needed some assistance with his marketing materials to promote his fantasy camp concept. Dad attended Randy's second camp that following January at the Cubs spring training facilities in Mesa. After that first camp he attended, he was hooked!

For a few years, there were two fantasy camps, one in January and one in April. When I was middle school age, my mother, younger sister, and I would attend the April camp with my father when it coincided with our Spring Break. It was always great to be able to escape to the warmer weather in Arizona.

Once my high school and college playing days were over, I couldn't wait to be 30 years old and play with my father in Randy's Cubs Fantasy Camp. My dream to play at camp with my father came true and I cherish all the times playing baseball with him. It became our Gaul family Field of Dreams. *When my boys, Alexander and Hunter, were younger, my wife Linda and I would make it our yearly family vacation. We all looked forward to being in sunny Mesa, Arizona, playing baseball. After camp each day my boys would join me for a little family catch and batting practice.*

I cannot forget a really great experience at Randy's 25ᵗʰ anniversary of his fantasy camps in 2008. I was in the locker room having lunch between games, and it was Ernie Banks's birthday. Rock star Eddie Vedder was there with Ernie discussing how Eddie needed to write a new Cubs song for Ernie's birthday. That evening Eddie wrote the song "All the Way" and we all were fortunate to see Eddie perform it for the first time at the camp banquet. Eddie's song for Ernie Banks became a popular song, especially during the Cubs' 2016 World Series Championship run. It's priceless things like this that truly made the camps special.

After reading Jerry's letter, I recall watching that entire song experience unfold for Ernie. Afterward, Eddie gifted me with the handwritten lyrics for the song and the guitar it was played on. Turns out, Eddie is as good a ballplayer as he is a musician.

Eddie Vedder

Then, there is this from Bob Madura…

After much procrastination, I arrived in Mesa, Arizona, in January of 2005 not really knowing what to expect. Little did I know that evening that my rookie year would see two "historic" events in the history of the Randy Hundley Fantasy Baseball Camp. The teams were announced and I learned that my coaches for that "Rookie Year" were going to be Rick "Big Daddy" Reuschel and Steve "Rainbow" Trout. It was a unique camp that year with many father/son combos and one father/daughter combo. Our team had three of them.

Entering the locker room on Monday was an awesome sight. Each cubicle had a camper's name placard over it with a blue pinstripe uniform and assorted accessories hanging there. I quickly learned that each section of the locker room had one or two former Cubs, sprinkled in between the returning veteran campers, and the rookies and I had the privilege of having a future Hall of Famer, Lee Smith, sitting right across from me. Monday started as each of the next five days would, with a camp meeting (AKA bull session), with the pros telling a few stories, field assignments, then to the fields for some stretching, a round of batting practice, and finally two seven-inning games separated by a carb-heavy lunch break. I quickly learned that I was best suited for pitching, but not in the traditional sense. It was feeding balls into the pitching machine to be exact.

Someone's gotta do it.

I clearly recall that on Tuesday, the clubhouse began to acquire a familiar fragrance about it. The smell of Bengay, Icy Hot, and whatever other balms the campers were self-"medicating" with, plus the industrial-strength ointments the trainers were using, permeated the air. A lot of moans and groans were heard, which would be the soundtrack for the rest of the week.

If there was one player/coach that was greatly beloved by all, it was the legendary Hall of Famer Ron Santo. If a camper came up to Ron and said anything like "My (insert relationship here) just was diagnosed with juvenile diabetes," he would ask if the camper had a cell phone with him and if could he get the individual on the phone. He would spend as much time as needed conversing with the person. It's that kind of thing that endeared Santo to millions of Cubs fans.

Then there was the daily ritual of "Kangaroo Court," where campers were taken to task for errors and other miscues on the field. Sometimes it was their own coaches and at times it may have been an opposing coach. The commentary and jeers resembled any celebrity roast that you may have seen. The fines for infractions (real or imagined) all went to a charitable cause, JDRF.

We could hardly wait for Saturday to arrive, and "The Big Game" that pits the campers vs. the pros. Both teams lined up down the baselines, the National Anthem was sung, and it was "Play Ball!"

The campers are the visiting team, batting in the top of the inning. Each camper team bats in the order of their record during the week. Rick had dubbed us "Da Bums." We had set a dubious camp record that year, being the first team to ever go 0–10. We knew we were going to the plate last, which gave me plenty of time to watch from the dugout — a very cool perspective.

It was a real defensive battle that year. The campers were leading 26–23 going into the 8th inning. Da Bums managed to eke out two more runs so the campers went into the bottom of the 8th with a five-run lead and Randy urging the pros on by shouting one of his favorite phrases, "Hey, we've got to strap it on!"

The pros have Willie Wilson leading off, and he hits a pop-up to our shortstop, John Rothchild. Keith Moreland grounds out to the second baseman, Rob Estka. The cheering from the campers becomes intense. The last batter is Leon "Bull" Durham, who crushes one foul down the first base line. The next pitch he launches one to deep center field, and we all hold our collective breath until Beth Chaplin hauls it and gets mobbed by the entire camp as the campers beat the pros for the first time in the then 23-year history of the camp, 28–23. Amazing experience, to say the least!

Comedian Mark DeCarlo was a two-time camper. Once for a 2010 television pilot called *Tripping Out* that had him on the road in various adventures and the second time as a full-fledged rookie, without the cameras.

I just tried my best to fit in, but it's an overwhelming experience for a Chicago boy. There's a couple of memories that stand out. The first was hitting two grand slams off the pitching machine, which is not as easy as it looks (at least that's what I tell people.) The second was during a lunch break, when everyone left for chow. I was with my brother Mike when we noticed Hall of Famer Billy Williams picking up baseballs in the outfield. We hustled out to help him bag balls and ended up skipping lunch and having a private batting lesson with a Cubs legend. Truly incredible. Field of Dreams *is more than a movie, it's a very real thing for me. Thanks, Randy!*

Finally, WGN Radio host Bob Sirott was at the camp in 1983 and recalled his experience…and more.

Randy, I can clearly remember being in the stands at Wrigley when you made your triumphant return to Chicago in 1976. I had snuck down to the box seats, and while I wasn't very happy you were wearing #4, it was a homecoming in every way. When you hit a double in your first at-bat, I was part of the standing ovation! I had no idea then that less than a decade later I would be suiting up at the fantasy camp for a TV special called "I Don't Care If I Ever Get Back." That week in Mesa was truly a legendary experience. Besides the aches and pains, foul tips and strains, I found myself in the presence of baseball royalty. A few memories really stand out. Like the late, great Ron Santo spending 45 minutes with me in the batting cage, helping to even out my swing. When I finally started to drive the ball, Santo beamed like a proud papa! Or the time I tried to stretch a single into a double and had the ugliest slide in the history of the game at second base. And the time I was in the batter's box, with Fergie on the mound. You were telling me exactly where the pitch would be, but by the time I figured it out, it was already in your mitt, and I was riding the pine. But the greatest memory I have was sitting in the locker next to "Mr. Cub" Ernie Banks for an entire week! Talking about baseball and life with a pioneer of the game, a hero of mine, was a surreal experience, one made possible by you and the genius of the camp concept. Years later, when Ernie passed, I attended his funeral and at one point you turned to me and said, "He'd love that you are here, Bob."

I was so honored to hear those words.

Every time we have had the chance to connect, be it at Wrigley in 1984 with you and Glenn Beckert (when you climbed up the grandstand supports to view the throngs of fans outside the stadium) for CBS News or sitting down one-on-one on the Marquee Sports Network talking about the 1969 team, or watching the Cubs beat the Dodgers to clinch the NL pennant, putting them into the 2016 World Series with you and some of the other Cubs, I always come away with a greater sense of the game, your place in it, and the absolute love that Chicago has for you as our ironman.

Locker partners Banks and Sirott

I am humbled by these letters and memories and am truly amazed at what the fantasy camp has done for me personally all these years. Some campers attend numerous times (some in excess of 25+ camps), and knowing they have integrated the experience into their lives in ways I could have never imagined is amazing to me when I think back to that parking lot discussion with Rich Melman. I will say that it didn't take long for the sting of not being able to coach in the majors to leave me when I had so many eager baseball fans who were fulfilling their childhood dreams of being on the diamond with their heroes while pulling muscles, pushing a single into a double, stealing a base, or even hitting a grand slam (albeit off a pitching machine) while wearing Cubbie blue.

An unintended side effect of the camp experience was that my former teammates, as well as other players, all got the chance to relive their own pro careers for a week, coaching and connecting with fans who they could help mold into ballplayers. To a player, every one of them came away with a remembered appreciation of the game and the importance of it to the campers. The list of names that participated includes some of the greats like Andy Pafko, who played 17 seasons in the majors (including the Cubs from 1943 to 1951) and was named to the Chicago Cubs All-Century Team. Hall of Famer "Mr. Cub" Ernie Banks, who needs no further introduction, and Jimmy Piersall, who also played 17 seasons, and was best known for his well-publicized battle with bipolar disorder that became the subject of a book and a film, *Fear Strikes Out*. The great Jody Davis, who led that 1984 Cubs team from behind the plate (and was the only other Cubs catcher in history to win a Gold Glove). Ron Santo, our captain and Hall of Famer, as well as Fergie Jenkins and Billy Williams, who are also enshrined in Cooperstown, as well as Ryne Sandberg and Lee Smith. Then you have those names in the Chicago Cubs Hall of Fame, including Glenn Beckert, Don Kessinger, Rick Sutcliffe, and José Cardenal.

There was also room for the guys who rounded out other great Cubs teams over the years, like Keith "Zonk" Moreland, Paul Popovich, Gary "Sarge" Matthews, Kerry Woods, Ron Coomer (who is now in the broadcast booth with Pat Hughes on radio), Bobby Dernier, Mike Tyson, Larry Biittner, Gene Hiser, and even my son, Todd, who put on the gear one more time for the camp.

The antics on and off the field are legendary. Watching the coaches put their teams through drills was a thing of beauty. My great friend Gene Oliver had become my right-hand man for the camps and had put on more than a few pounds by this point in his life. Watching Ollie trying to run alongside his campers, huffing and puffing, was like seeing a thundering rhino wearing a baseball jersey, as his rookies were doing their best to maintain their composure. During the morning meetings when I introduced the day's sessions, the mood was pretty laid back, until Joe Pepitone would jump up with a bat, take his neatly combed hairpiece off, throw it up in the air like it was skeet, and pretend the bat was a shotgun to shoot it out of sky. Then he'd stomp on it, and put it back on, and take a bow. Santo was always up for a laugh, as was Beckert and the two of them would gang up on me, but it was all in good fun. Being back in uniform with so many of my friends gave us all another drink at the fountain of youth. We didn't look or move the same as we did back in the day, but inside, the fire was still there.

We always closed camp with a great evening event, handing out those million-dollar contracts to all the campers, a signed baseball by the pros, and eventually, in later years some, great entertainment by the late comedian Royce Elliot, who had everyone in stitches.

When that second camp ended, I knew there was no turning back, and I ended up quitting my investment banking job to focus full time on the fantasy camp concept. In addition to the Cubs, I eventually ran camps for the Cardinals, White Sox, Yankees, and Angels. I ended up with an office and a small staff to handle it all and loved every single minute of it.

We've had men and women from all walks of life attend camp. Everyone from teachers to lawyers, police officers to businesspeople, retired military to celebs—Phil Donahue, actor John Cusak, and Chicago Blackhawks star Chris Chelios have all worn Cubbie blue and given their best at camp. But the day that rock star Eddie Vedder, a lifelong Cubs fan, signed up to wear the pinstripes just goes to prove that you can be a huge celebrity and adored by millions, but for that little kid inside, having a catch in a big-league uniform, stepping on the green grass under a blue sky, and waiting for the next pitch, fly ball, or line drive, is the stuff dreams are made of.

All the camps have been special to me, but the most emotional one was held in Dyersville, Iowa, where the movie *Field of Dreams* was filmed. The movie goes right to the heart of baseball, and that special bond between a father and son that endures through the ages. I was near tears most of the time, thinking about my own dad, of course, and how much he would have loved to be in the middle of all that corn, and have a catch.

The fantasy camps were very much a *"build it and they will come"* dream of mine that came true many times over. I'm so grateful to the fans and former players who created some unforgettable memories. After 38 years, Covid-19 knocked the fantasy camps off the map in 2021, and it's been extremely difficult to find a way to play ball again. Thousands of campers are waiting to see if there will be a comeback of sorts, another opportunity for them to wear the blue pinstripes of their beloved Chicago Cubs, to spend a week in Arizona or a few days at Wrigley Field, hanging out with their baseball heroes, and living the field of dreams experience one more time.

Baseball in so many ways is a time machine, and it's been my high honor to keep the camps going all these years. It's one thing to watch the game and quite another to play it, and even though I had stellar seasons with the Cubs, the Randy Hundley Fantasy Camps are on par with my pro baseball achievements. I am so very proud to represent the Chicago Cubs as the originator of the fantasy camps and to keep the great legacy of the organization alive in my own way with thousands of fans over the years.

Fantasy Camp 2020

-12-
EXTRA INNINGS

It's getting late in the game for me. I don't know where the time has gone.

It seems like just yesterday I was a fresh-faced kid out of Martinsville, looking for my place in the big leagues. But the truth is, I've just turned 81 years old, and I feel every bloomin' inch of it most days. Over the years all the physical activity and injuries from baseball have taken their toll on me, causing me to change out my original parts for new ones, including my knees, hips, and shoulders. Last year, I had serious surgery to open up a severely clogged artery in my heart. The recovery has knocked me back on my hillbilly fanny more than I thought it would, but I keep taking steps back toward better health. Working on this book has me missing my dad in a big way, but also very blessed that my mom is still with us and, as of this writing, is 101 years old.

However, the biggest difficulty I've had to face is life without Betty for the past 23 years. In 1989, we were on our return trip home from watching Todd play in an All-Star game in West Virginia when she told me that she needed to stop at the doctor's office to get some test results. We found out that she had breast cancer. I remember telling my kids Renee and Chad (who were on the trip with us) that we could have an hour to cry and be sad and then we would start to fight like all get-out. She battled back, and it went into remission, but it returned in 1997.

Betty passed away on September 4, 2000, at the age of 58.

From that day on, the light has gone out of my life on so many levels. Her faith was so strong that it lingers to this day, and I often feel her presence with me, even though physically she is no longer here. She's missed so much by our family and it's a deep hole that is often hard for me to dig out of at times, as it is for our kids. Just a few months after Betty passed away, our son, Todd, signed on with the Chicago Cubs, something she and I spoke about often. It was hard not to have her with us when the announcement was made that the Hundley legacy continued at Wrigley Field, but I guess it wasn't meant to be. Betty was a great believer, and while most days I still feel like a man who is missing half of his body, I know that she is with her Lord, and I take a measure of comfort in that.

Even so, I wish she was here with me, for there is so much I'd like to share with her. We had more than a marriage; we had an unseen bond that held us together. Our roots go back to those early days at Bassett High School, and countless memories that sprouted the branches of a sacred family tree that, in turn, made for a powerful life together. Betty was the rock of our family. Her deep reservoir of love was poured onto me and our children, and since the day she passed away, there have been more times than I can count where I have held on to that love in order to keep myself upright and moving forward. This loss could be crippling if I allow it to be. I know that she would insist I live my life in a way that honors the one we had together, and every day I make every attempt to do just that.

In the previous chapter, I shared just a small slice of the fantasy camp experience, and during the years since Betty's passing, the campers who attended, as well as so many of my teammates, surrounded me with great affection and support during the most difficult time of my life. The same goes for the legions of Cubs fans who reached out with their condolences.

Your thoughts and prayers have meant the world to me.

The loss of my former teammates has also been difficult. I've played with some incredible ballplayers over the years, and so many of them mentioned in this book became brothers to me.

I feel fortunate to have had some extra innings in life that they didn't get a chance to play. But saying goodbye to them has been a sobering reminder that tomorrow is promised to none of us.

****

On December 3, 2010, I got a call from Ron Santo Jr. telling me that his dad had passed away. I'd been planning a visit to see Ronnie and was shocked to get the news, even though I knew that his lifelong battle with diabetes had taken a serious toll. My memories of #10 both, on and off the field, are of a fun-loving guy who'd give you the shirt off his back if need be. In so many ways he was the face of the Chicago Cubs. This hard-nosed third baseman who carried the team on his shoulders for so many years had a deep enthusiasm for the game that was self-evident. Years after his playing days were over, from 1996 to 2010, radio listeners would be witnesses to his boyish energy, as he wore his heart on his sleeve for millions of fans in Cubs nation as he sat in the broadcast booth alongside the great Hall of Fame broadcaster Pat Hughes. Their close friendship and on-air chemistry became known as *The Pat and Ron Show,* and you never knew what would come out of Ronnie's mouth, but it was always in support of his beloved Cubs.

On a side note, I was originally offered the color commentary seat, but when I met with the execs, I told them I wouldn't do beer commercials or liquor endorsements. That was the end of my broadcasting career. But, as it turned out, Ronnie was the right guy for the job.

Ron Santo was the first player in MLB history to play the game with Type 1 diabetes. When he was diagnosed at the age of 18, the average life expectancy for a person with Type 1 diabetes was only 25 years. I have always thought this knowledge of limited time was the source of his great love of the game and people. In the early years, Ron kept his condition to himself, fearing that he'd be forced out of the game he loved so much if anyone found out. Often, he'd sneak a candy bar before hitting, just to make sure he had the energy to get in the batter's box. Turning a negative into a positive, he would become a powerful advocate for the Juvenile Diabetes Research Foundation, helping to raise millions of dollars in search of a cure that he knew might not help him, but might alleviate the suffering of others. Ron lost both of his legs to diabetes, but he never let it slow him down, and since 1979, the annual Ron Santo Walk to Cure Diabetes in Chicago has raised over $65 million for the organization. It is a fitting legacy to a great player, friend, and teammate.

At his funeral, Ernie, Fergie, Beck, Billy, and I carried the coffin of our friend. It was draped with a flag with #10 on it, the same flag that had flown over Wrigley on the day his number was retired in 2003. Two years after he passed, Ron Santo was inducted into the Baseball Hall of Fame in Cooperstown. Ron's son Jeff produced an excellent documentary about his father called *This Old Cub* which I highly recommend and is the perfect tribute to one of the greatest to ever wear a Cubs uniform.

Hall of Famers Ron Santo & Ernie Banks

Five years after Ron died, we lost the legendary Ernie Banks on January 23, 2015. "Mr. Cub" is regarded by many as one of the greatest ballplayers of all time. I can tell you from personal experience, that's true, but it was his presence off the field that made him one of the all-time greats. He was the first Cubs player to be awarded a Gold Glove, and he was inducted into Cooperstown in 1977 and was named to the Major League Baseball All-Century Team in 1999. Ernie's quiet leadership was a major part of our baseball success, and to be there when he hit his 500th home run was something I will never forget. In 1982, the Cubs retired Ernie Banks's #14, the first one in franchise history. His flag hangs right alongside Ronnie's at Wrigley Field, and on March 31, 2008, a statue of Ernie was unveiled in front of Wrigley Field.

After Ernie's funeral service, the procession went right past Wrigley Field for one last nod to the man who changed the game of baseball on so many levels.

Nineteen players from the 1969 team have passed away. Besides Ron and Ernie, I've said goodbye to Jim Hickman, Glenn Beckert, Willie Smith, Oscar Gamble, my side-kick Gene Oliver, Manny Jimenez, Charley Smith, Randy Bobb, Bill Hands, Dick Selma, Ted Abernathy, Joe Niekro, Hank Aguirre, Ken Johnson, Joe Decker, Don Nottebart, and Alec Distaso. Joe Pepitone passed away during the writing of this book, and even though Pepi wasn't on the '69 team, his presence was unforgettable, just like the late Milt Pappas, who died in 2016.

My memories of Ron, Ernie, Beck, Ollie, Hick, Oscar, and the rest of the boys are solid gold. In my mind, we are locked in as we were back then—invincible young men, playing the game we loved. Ron, Ollie, and Beck were always a big part of the fantasy camp experience. One of the great, wonderful side effects of the experience was rekindling the friendships we all shared during our playing days.

****

At 90 years old Al Spangler is the oldest living Cubs player from the 1969 team. Fergie and Kessinger are 80, Paul Popovich and Nate Oliver are 82, and Bill Heath is 84. Billy Williams is 85; Jimmie Hall and "The Vulture" Phil Reagan are 86 years old. We still have some youngsters who are still living their lives long after they hung up their cleats. Dave Lemonds is 74, Gary Ross is 75, and Ken Rudolph is 76, as are Jimmy Qualls and Rick Bladt. Ken Holtzman, Archie Reynolds, Don Young, and Jim Colborn are all 77 years old. Rich Nye and Johnny Hairston are both 79.

The only coach left from that team who is still with us is Joey Almalfitano, who is 89. Pete Reiser, Rube Walker, Joe Becker, and of course, Leo Durocher, have all passed on. The great broadcasters from that era, Jack Brickhouse and Lou Boudreau, as well as Lloyd Pettit and Vince Lloyd, who brought the games to life on both television and radio, are no longer with us. Pat Pieper, "The Voice of Wrigley Field," passed away in 1974. Time has erased much of that glorious, yet bittersweet, '69 season, when we set the world on fire and brought baseball back to "The Friendly Confines" in the finest form possible.

****

I also want to take a moment here to acknowledge and thank the chairman of the Chicago Cubs, Tom Ricketts. He knows what it's like to sit through losing seasons watching from the bleachers, long before his family became the owners of the ball club in 2009. He spent his share of time back in the day at the Sports Corner Bar & Grill across the street from Wrigley Field and actually lived above the bar after graduating from the University of Chicago. He met his wife, Cecelia, in the bleachers, and as a teen memorized Ryne Sandberg's stats from his 1984 MVP season. The early seasons after the Ricketts' family acquired the team were turbulent, but they set the right path with Theo Epstein and, of course, created the lineup which broke "The Curse of the Billy Goat" in 2016 by winning the World Series. As a former player, my chest swelled with pride watching Rizzo, Bryant, Schwarber, Lester, Ross, Arietta, Báez, manager Joe Maddon, and the rest of the players continue to build on the foundation that so many of us put in place for them years ago.

In April of 2017, a group of former Cubs players were given World Series rings in recognition of our dedication to the organization over the years. I was so fortunate to receive a ring, along with Fergie Jenkins, Billy Williams, Glenn Beckert, José Cardenal, Ryne Sandberg, Jody Davis, Bob Dernier, Scott Sanderson, Lee Smith, and Steve Trout. There were posthumous rings for Ernie Banks and Ron Santo as well. While I never made it to the postseason in my career, being inducted into the Chicago Cubs Hall of Fame in 1984 has meant the world to me.

I sure wish Betty could have been here for the ring ceremony with me, and it would have been great to slip the big ring on her finger. My baseball career and the legacy I have carved out in the game wouldn't exist without her in my life. I take great pride in wearing the ring everywhere I go, and of course, it becomes a point of conversation with fans, whom I gladly let wear it (as long as they give it back) and take as many pic-

**2016 World Series ring presentation with
Tom Ricketts and Crane Kenney**

tures as they want. They too, are a big part of Chicago Cubs history and have stood by the team through some very bad years and some incredible ones. They were more like an extended family than fans. Nearly 50 years since I retired from baseball, I am still stopped by fans who want to share their memories of what the Cubs have meant to them over the years, and to tell me how much they appreciated our efforts both on and off the field. The life I have lived has far exceeded those dreams I had as a boy. I am proud of my place in the history of the game, blessed by the men that I had the chance to play with, and astounded that so many years after I retired, Cubs fans still remember me and for that, I am so very grateful.

Thank you for being part of my life and allowing me to be a part of yours.

Randy Hundley

AFTERWORD

BY JOHN ST. AUGUSTINE

When Randy asked me to assist him in writing his story, the answer was an immediate and resounding YES! For me, it was a serious full-circle moment and one that I don't think even he was aware of when we started this project together, shortly after his 80th birthday.

Back in 1967 one of my favorite things to do was play catch in the backyard of my grandmother's house, a place that we had just moved from a year before. It was a serious upheaval for an eight-year-old boy because that meant I wouldn't be able to see my best friend, Garry, who lived down the block anymore. However, every Saturday morning my dad would take the short ride back to our old home to check on his mom, and I'd stand out in front of Garry's house, bellowing for him to come out. Then we'd race to my gram's huge backyard, and we'd run through an entire Cubs game with Garry pitching (usually as Fergie Jenkins, he had the leg kick down), and I was behind the plate as "The Rebel." Garry had a glove but I didn't, so I fashioned my ballcap as a mitt, and since we used a rubber ball, it didn't hurt too much.

We played endless hours of catch this way until it was too dark to see the ball.

Our new home was just three blocks away from the corner of Berteau and Keeler Avenue in Chicago. It was an intersection with a stop sign that the Cubs players had to maneuver before they hit the Kennedy Expressway on their way home to the suburbs. For decades, kids waited on every corner on the route from Wrigley, but our corner *was the last one* and the final chance to get an autograph. Hundley, Santo, Beckert, and others always signed whatever we offered, be it a ball, piece of paper, or someone's arm.

Two years later, in the summer of '69, I was caught up in Cubs Fever, as they battled for baseball dominance. However, our heroes came up short, and the fog of losing it all after that magical summer shrouded the Windy City. I was heartbroken, just like the rest of the Cubs fans. But it was during a seventh-inning rainout against the fledgling Montreal Expos in 1970 that changed everything. As I watched on TV the fans began to make their way out of the park, so I made my way out the door. Just a few minutes later, I was standing on the corner of Berteau and Keeler, beneath a humongous oak tree trying to keep dry. All the required tools were on hand: a new pen, my official Randy Hundley catcher's mitt, and a small address book that was filled with autographs. I waited. A good twenty minutes went by before I realized that there would be no competition for autographs that day. As the rain intensified, the fair-weather fans stayed home, and I had the corner all to myself! I kept a keen eye open for any telltale signs that the drivers who stopped at the crosswalk on their way to the expressway might be Cubs players.

All the neighborhood kids knew that Glenn Beckert sometimes wore a sailor-type hat with the sides down and that Ron Santo often sported mirrored shades. Some cars had a sticker that indicated they parked in the players' lot and were not mere mortals. A few guys came by and waved in my direction with a look on their faces that said, "Is this kid nuts standing around in the rain?" Almost an hour elapsed, and I figured it was time to hang it up for the day. I was 0–3, with no autographs, handshakes, or high-fives. As I turned to leave, my eyes caught a flash of red heading my way. It was a Corvette with CUBS9 on the front plate! As the muscle car came closer, I could see it was Randy Hundley!

Randy pulled his car over to the curb and the window came down real slow. *"What in the Sam Hill are you doing standing out in this storm for, boy?"* he drawled in his thick Virginia accent. With my knees knocking and body shivering from both the downpour and the fact that the greatest catcher in the history of Earth was an arm's length away, I said something like, "Waiting for an autograph, sir." The next few minutes were a blur. "Get in, son. You're going to catch your death of cold." There I sat in the car, staring in amazement as Hundley signed the mitt and address book, while I dripped all over his leather seats.

"Where do you live?" he asked.

"Right up the street."

"Then get going, kid, or you'll miss supper!"

I hopped out on his orders, and Hundley made a hard left turn and was off to the races. I stood there not knowing what to do.

No one was going to believe that I had sat in "The Rebel's" Corvette! I burned rubber on my Red Ball Jets all the way home, went up to my room, and sat on the bed. I was soaked to the bone, but I pounded a ball into the newly signed mitt and I think it was my pillow that night, even though I hardly slept.

****

Twenty-two years later, I got a call to cover the Randy Hundley Fantasy Camps for the long-gone *Chicago Sports Profiles Magazine*. It was my first paid writing gig, even though I cannot recall how it all happened. I couldn't believe I was getting a check for $250 *and* playing baseball with the guys whose autographs I used to wait hours for! When I got to the first day of camp, I started sharing the corner story with Randy, but instead of listening, he looked at me and barked, *"Start running laps, rookie!"*

As you have read, the camp experience was unforgettable.

The moment I hit a grand slam at UIC Field and saw Gene Oliver and my teammates waiting for me at home plate is an image burned into my mind. The 10-year-old boy inside me still can't believe it. About a month later, Randy called to thank me for writing such a great article, and we've been friends ever since.

I've had a great career in broadcasting, as well as being an author, and over the past nine years have either ghostwritten, coached, or published books for people with a story to tell that would most likely never be recognized by a traditional publisher.

While all those projects had value, this one is personal for me.

Perhaps you have heard of the book *Tuesdays with Morrie* by Mitch Albom? Well, this was *Wednesdays with Randy*, as we'd go out to breakfast, where I'd watch him put more pepper on his food than any other person I know, and talk about the book concept. Then I'd be witness to legions of Cubs fans, young and old, gravitate to him like a magnet. His presence and voice are unmistakable. Over and over again he'd take pictures, sign autographs, answer questions, and let people wear his 2016 World Series ring given to him by the Cubs. Afterward, we'd go to his home, clear the kitchen table and I'd set up microphones. There we sat hour after hour as Randy shared stories from his life. The glorious moments, and the tragic ones, and stories from a time when baseball was more of a game and less of a business. The characters he shared the field with, his long route to the majors, and his deep love of the game. He was recovering from major surgery during this time, but he toughed it out, as he always has. Those stories and memories created the foundation of the book. Add to that, a few hundred hours of researching stats, online sources, and newspapers from the 20th century, and I'm proud of our tag-team efforts in sharing Randy's life story.

Supporting my friend throughout this book-writing process has been a high honor and my way to thank him for all the joy he's given me and Cubs fans over the years.

By the way, all these decades later, that red Corvette is still in Randy's driveway, and I can't help but give it a little tap on the passenger side door every time I have the chance. The car door window reflects a much older face, but the kid inside me still can't believe that the baseball gods saw fit to have me be part of bringing this book alive and telling the story of one of the great catchers, innovators, competitors, and gentlemen in the long and storied history of the Chicago Cubs.

Thanks, Coach!

John St. Augustine

Fantasy Camp 1993—Wrigley Field

THANKS TO THESE GREAT CUB FANS
FOR MAKING *IRONMAN* POSSIBLE!

Garry Prange

Jack Stanis

Matt Kelly

Ron Zagorski

Eric Levy

John Keith

Judy Zuckweiler

Tim Anderson

Jonathon Augustine

Tom Voegtle

Jeff Conrad

The Lynch Family

David Hirsch

Diane Geiser

Geoff & Patricia Munro

Steve Jansen

Kevin Clark

Johnny Nino

Gail Cannova

Pat Bresnahan

Charlie Janus

Dick Neubauer

Christina Pentrancosta

Eric Soderholm

Colleen Craine

Jake Asplund

Bill Kurtis &
Donna LaPietra

Mike Devine

Tadhg Devine

Jim Malinski

Patty Andres

"Big Steve"
Kendziorski

Patrick Shine

Joe Petrungaro

Sue Land

Vinny Connor

Rob Smith

Kathy Grossmann

Susan Kowlakowski

Chuck & Candace
Jordan

Osvaldo Cruz Jr.

Patty Viera

Martin Valdez

Dan Coughlan

Mark Ruffin

Jerry Niewiadomski

Joe Niewiadomski

Shawn McGovern

Frank Preo

Jim Clark

Rich Hoffman

Debi Daniels

Kim Munro

Roger Schenck

John Stevens

Shellie Hall

Tim Evans

Sue Brown

Pete Miceli

Jim Miceli

Barb Ogorek

Gary Smith

Dennis Kijowski

Tricia Wetherell

Marcy Rubin

Brian Smith

Dreams of Hope Ranch

Jan & Scott Jansen

Michael C. Reid

Tim Moeller

Brian, Barb, Keegan &
Kelly McCaskey

James F. Rooney

THE RANDY HUNDLEY FANTASY CAMPERS!

Beth Chaplin	Mark DeCarlo	Steve Weinberg
Dave Chaplin	Dave Horn	Bryan "Red" Redington
Bob Madura	Hank Smith	Sam Goodman
Paul Lawrence	Mark Smith	Bob Sirott
Ron Hoyle	Karl Marquardt	Andrew DeLorenzo
Don Bino	Cliff Gray	Jeff Pavlik
Bob Farinelli	Jerry Gaul	David L. "Doc" Fishman
Scott Marks	Kris McClearn	
Ron Wexler	John & Robin Salzeider	Zak Fishman
David Wexler	Steve Mahon	Royce Tharp
Justin Wexler	Robin Peterson	Carl Helfrich
Jacyn Wexler	Brad Cohen	Bob Kulefsky
Daniel Klein	Bill Thomas	Rich Kulefsky
Jeff Horn	Mickey Martin	Ernie Koehler
		Alison Koehler

IN MEMORY OF THESE BLEACHER SITTING, W FLAG WAVING, CUB FANS!

Molly Creely	Emmerson Munro	Marge Nino
Joey Stock	Kevin Mallehan	Paul Schubitz
Dorothy Stevens	Bob Annis	Arni Cohen
John "JC" Coleman	Chuck Mahon	Alice Dust
Lenny "Ace" Carlson	Wayne Hall	Debbie Evans-Gibson
James B. Novello	Charles Serafino	Donna Zagorski
Christopher McQuillen	Bobby Merens	John & Carol Augustine

ABOUT THE AUTHORS

Cecil Randolph Hundley Jr.

Nicknamed "The Rebel," Randy Hundley was the field general for the Chicago Cubs under manager Leo Durocher and became one of the game's biggest stars with his durability, leadership, and skills behind the plate. The Virginia native played 10 seasons with the Cubs in the 1960s and 1970s and was considered a leader on the field for the team that endured a historic collapse in 1969. Hundley led National League catchers in putouts and won the 1967 National League Gold Glove Award for catchers as the Cubs improved from a last-place finish in 1966 to finish in third place. Hundley set a major league record in 1968 with 160 appearances behind the plate and caught more than 90 percent of all Cubs games from 1966 to 1969. Hundley also introduced the one-handed catching style, a technique that Hall of Fame catcher Johnny Bench and other catchers soon copied. Upon retiring after the 1977 season and managing 3½ years in the minor leagues, Hundley established baseball fantasy camps for adults that ran for 38 years. He was inducted into the Cubs Hall of Fame in 1984, and in 2016, Hundley was awarded a World Series ring for his lifelong efforts both on and off the field from the Chicago Cubs.

John St. Augustine

John has earned the reputation as one of the premiere talk radio hosts in America for his intense delivery and interviewing skills and is a three-time winner of the Michigan Association of Broadcasters Best Talk Host Award. John created the initial concept for *Oprah Radio*, and in 2006 became the creator and senior producer of *The Dr. Oz Show, The Jean Chatzky Show,* and *The Bob Greene Show* on the Sirius XM channel. John also created and hosted the Peabody Award–nominated Sirius Radio program *John Denver Remembered: The Man and His Music*. He is the creator and executive producer of *Earth Matters with Bill Kurtis* and the *Life 2.0 Podcast*. Additionally, John is the bestselling author of *Living an Uncommon Life, Every Moment Matters,* and *Phenomena*. He is also a sought-after literary coach and audiobook producer and has two TEDx talks to his credit.

John's website is www.auroramediaproductions.com.